Incoterms® 2010

ICC rules
for the use of domestic and
international trade terms

Entry into force: 1 January 2011

ICC Services
Publications
38 Cours Albert 1er
75008 Paris
France

ICC United Kingdom
The British affiliate of ICC
12 Grosvenor Place
London, SW1X 7HH
United Kingdom

ICC Publication No. 715E
ISBN: 978-92-842-0080-1

www.iccbooks.com

www.iccbookshop.com

CONTENTS

INCOTERMS® 2010

FOREWORD

By Rajat Gupta, ICC Chairman

The global economy has given businesses broader access than ever before to markets all over the world. Goods are sold in more countries, in larger quantities, and in greater variety. But as the volume and complexity of global sales increase, so do possibilities for misunderstandings and costly disputes when sale contracts are not adequately drafted.

The Incoterms® rules, the ICC rules on the use of domestic and international trade terms, facilitate the conduct of global trade. Reference to an Incoterms® 2010 rule in a sale contract clearly defines the parties' respective obligations and reduces the risk of legal complications.

Since the creation of the Incoterms rules by ICC in 1936, this globally accepted contractual standard has been regularly updated to keep pace with the development of international trade. The Incoterms® 2010 rules take account of the continued spread of customs-free zones, the increased use of electronic communications in business transactions, heightened concern about security in the movement of goods and changes in transport practices. *Incoterms® 2010* updates and consolidates the 'delivered' rules, reducing the total number of rules from 13 to 11, and offers a simpler and clearer presentation of all the rules. *Incoterms® 2010* is also the first version of the Incoterms rules to make all references to buyers and sellers gender-neutral.

The broad expertise of ICC's Commission on Commercial Law and Practice, whose membership is drawn from all parts of the world and all trade sectors, ensures that the Incoterms® 2010 rules respond to business needs everywhere.

ICC would like to express its gratitude to the members of the Commission, chaired by Fabio Bortolotti (Italy), to the Drafting Group, which comprised Charles Debattista (Co-Chair, UK), Christoph Martin Radtke (Co-Chair, France), Jens Bredow (Germany), Johnny Herre (Sweden), David Lowe (UK), Lauri Railas (Finland), Frank Reynolds (US), and Miroslav Subert (Czech Republic), and to Asko Raty (Finland) for assistance with the images depicting the 11 rules.

INTRODUCTION

The Incoterms®[1] rules explain a set of three-letter trade terms reflecting business-to-business practice in contracts for the sale of goods. The Incoterms rules describe mainly the tasks, costs and risks involved in the delivery of goods from sellers to buyers.

How to use the Incoterms® 2010 rules

1. Incorporate the Incoterms® 2010 rules into your contract of sale

If you want the Incoterms® 2010 rules to apply to your contract, you should make this clear in the contract, through such words as, "[*the chosen Incoterms rule including the named place, followed by*] Incoterms® 2010".

2. Choose the appropriate Incoterms rule

The chosen Incoterms rule needs to be appropriate to the goods, to the means of their transport, and above all to whether the parties intend to put additional obligations, for example such as the obligation to organize carriage or insurance, on the seller or on the buyer. The Guidance Note to each Incoterms rule contains information that is particularly helpful when making this choice. Whichever Incoterms rule is chosen, the parties should be aware that the interpretation of their contract may well be influenced by customs particular to the port or place being used.

3. Specify your place or port as precisely as possible

The chosen Incoterms rule can work only if the parties name a place or port, and will work best if the parties specify the place or port as precisely as possible.

A good example of such precision would be:

"FCA 38 Cours Albert 1er, Paris, France Incoterms® 2010".

Under the Incoterms rules Ex Works (EXW), Free Carrier (FCA), Delivered at Terminal (DAT), Delivered at Place (DAP), Delivered Duty Paid (DDP), Free Alongside Ship (FAS), and Free on Board (FOB), the named place is the place where delivery takes place and where risk passes from the seller to the buyer. Under the Incoterms rules Carriage Paid to (CPT), Carriage and Insurance Paid to (CIP), Cost and Freight (CFR) and Cost, Insurance and Freight (CIF), the named place differs from the place of delivery. Under these four Incoterms rules, the named

1."Incoterms" is a registered trademark of the International Chamber of Commerce.

place is the place of destination to which carriage is paid. Indications as to place or destination can helpfully be further specified by stating a precise point in that place or destination in order to avoid doubt or argument.

4. Remember that Incoterms rules do not give you a complete contract of sale

Incoterms rules *do* say which party to the sale contract has the obligation to make carriage or insurance arrangements, when the seller delivers the goods to the buyer, and which costs each party is responsible for. Incoterms rules, however, say nothing about the price to be paid or the method of its payment. Neither do they deal with the transfer of ownership of the goods, or the consequences of a breach of contract. These matters are normally dealt with through express terms in the contract of sale or in the law governing that contract. The parties should be aware that mandatory local law may override any aspect of the sale contract, including the chosen Incoterms rule.

Main features of the Incoterms® 2010 rules

1. Two new Incoterms rules – DAT and DAP – have replaced the Incoterms 2000 rules DAF, DES, DEQ and DDU

The number of Incoterms rules has been reduced from 13 to 11. This has been achieved by substituting two new rules that may be used irrespective of the agreed mode of transport – DAT, Delivered at Terminal, and DAP, Delivered at Place – for the Incoterms 2000 rules DAF, DES, DEQ and DDU.

Under both new rules, delivery occurs at a named destination: in DAT, at the buyer's disposal unloaded from the arriving vehicle (as under the former DEQ rule); in DAP, likewise at the buyer's disposal, but ready for unloading (as under the former DAF, DES and DDU rules).

The new rules make the Incoterms 2000 rules DES and DEQ superfluous. The named terminal in DAT may well be in a port, and DAT can therefore safely be used in cases where the Incoterms 2000 rule DEQ once was. Likewise, the arriving "vehicle" under DAP may well be a ship and the named place of destination may well be a port: consequently, DAP can safely be used in cases where the Incoterms 2000 rule DES once was. These new rules, like their predecessors, are "delivered", with the seller bearing all the costs (other than those related to import clearance, where applicable) and risks involved in bringing the goods to the named place of destination.

2. Classification of the 11 Incoterms® 2010 rules

The 11 Incoterms® 2010 rules are presented in two distinct classes:

RULES FOR ANY MODE OR MODES OF TRANSPORT

EXW EX WORKS

FCA FREE CARRIER

CPT CARRIAGE PAID TO
CIP CARRIAGE AND INSURANCE PAID TO

DAT DELIVERED AT TERMINAL
DAP DELIVERED AT PLACE
DDP DELIVERED DUTY PAID

RULES FOR SEA AND INLAND WATERWAY TRANSPORT

FAS FREE ALONGSIDE SHIP
FOB FREE ON BOARD

CFR COST AND FREIGHT
CIF COST INSURANCE AND FREIGHT

The first class includes the seven Incoterms® 2010 rules that can be used irrespective of the mode of transport selected and irrespective of whether one or more than one mode of transport is employed. EXW, FCA, CPT, CIP, DAT, DAP and DDP belong to this class. They can be used even when there is no maritime transport at all. It is important to remember, however, that these rules *can* be used in cases where a ship *is* used for part of the carriage.

In the second class of Incoterms® 2010 rules, the point of delivery and the place to which the goods are carried to the buyer are *both* ports, hence the label "sea and inland waterway" rules. FAS, FOB, CFR and CIF belong to this class. Under the last three Incoterms rules, all mention of the ship's rail as the point of delivery has been omitted in preference for the goods being delivered when they are "on board" the vessel. This more closely reflects modern commercial reality and avoids the rather dated image of the risk swinging to and fro across an imaginary perpendicular line.

3. Rules for domestic and international trade

Incoterms rules have traditionally been used in *international* sale contracts where goods pass across national borders. In various areas of the world, however, trade blocs, like the European Union, have made border formalities between different countries less significant. Consequently, the subtitle of the Incoterms® 2010 rules formally recognizes that they are available for application to both international and domestic sale contracts. As a result, the Incoterms® 2010 rules clearly state in a number of places that the obligation to comply with export/import formalities exists only where applicable.

Two developments have persuaded ICC that a movement in this direction is timely. Firstly, traders commonly use Incoterms rules for purely domestic sale contracts. The second reason is the greater willingness in the United States to use Incoterms rules in domestic trade rather than the former Uniform Commercial Code shipment and delivery terms.

4. Guidance Notes

Before each Incoterms® 2010 rule you will find a Guidance Note. The Guidance Notes explain the fundamentals of each Incoterms rule, such as when it should be used, when risk passes, and how costs are allocated between seller and buyer. The Guidance Notes are not part of the actual Incoterms® 2010 rules, but are intended to help the user accurately and efficiently steer towards the appropriate Incoterms rule for a particular transaction.

5. Electronic communication

Previous versions of Incoterms rules have specified those documents that could be replaced by EDI messages. Articles A1/B1 of the Incoterms® 2010 rules, however, now give electronic means of communication the same effect as paper communication, as long as the parties so agree or where customary. This formulation facilitates the evolution of new electronic procedures throughout the lifetime of the Incoterms® 2010 rules.

6. Insurance cover

The Incoterms® 2010 rules are the first version of the Incoterms rules since the revision of the Institute Cargo Clauses and take account of alterations made to those clauses. The Incoterms® 2010 rules place information duties relating to insurance in articles A3/B3, which deal with contracts of carriage and insurance. These provisions have been moved from the more generic articles found in articles A10/B10 of the

Incoterms 2000 rules. The language in articles A3/B3 relating to insurance has also been altered with a view to clarifying the parties' obligations in this regard.

7. Security-related clearances and information required for such clearances

There is heightened concern nowadays about security in the movement of goods, requiring verification that the goods do not pose a threat to life or property for reasons other than their inherent nature. Therefore, the Incoterms® 2010 rules have allocated obligations between the buyer and seller to obtain or to render assistance in obtaining security-related clearances, such as chain-of-custody information, in articles A2/B2 and A10/B10 of various Incoterms rules.

8. Terminal handling charges

Under Incoterms rules CPT, CIP, CFR, CIF, DAT, DAP, and DDP, the seller must make arrangements for the carriage of the goods to the agreed destination. While the freight is paid by the seller, it is actually paid *for* by the buyer as freight costs are normally included by the seller in the total selling price. The carriage costs will sometimes include the costs of handling and moving the goods within port or container terminal facilities and the carrier or terminal operator may well charge these costs to the buyer who receives the goods. In these circumstances, the buyer will want to avoid paying for the same service twice: once to the seller as part of the total selling price and once independently to the carrier or the terminal operator. The Incoterms® 2010 rules seek to avoid this happening by clearly allocating such costs in articles A6/B6 of the relevant Incoterms rules.

9. String sales

In the sale of commodities, as opposed to the sale of manufactured goods, cargo is frequently sold several times during transit "down a string". When this happens, a seller in the middle of the string does not "ship" the goods because these have already been shipped by the first seller in the string. The seller in the middle of the string therefore performs its obligations towards its buyer not by shipping the goods, but by "procuring" goods that have been shipped. For clarification purposes, Incoterms® 2010 rules include the obligation to "procure goods shipped" as an alternative to the obligation to ship goods in the relevant Incoterms rules.

Variants of Incoterms rules

Sometimes the parties want to alter an Incoterms rule. The Incoterms® 2010 rules do not prohibit such alteration, but there are dangers in so doing. In order to avoid any unwelcome surprises, the parties would need to make the intended effect of such alterations extremely clear in their contract. Thus, for example, if the allocation of costs in the Incoterms® 2010 rules is altered in the contract, the parties should also clearly state whether they intend to vary the point at which the risk passes from seller to buyer.

Status of this introduction

This introduction gives general information on the use and interpretation of the Incoterms® 2010 rules, but does not form part of those rules.

Explanation of terms used in the Incoterms® 2010 rules

As in the Incoterms 2000 rules, the seller's and buyer's obligations are presented in mirror fashion, reflecting under column A the seller's obligations and under column B the buyer's obligations. These obligations can be carried out personally by the seller or the buyer or sometimes, subject to terms in the contract or the applicable law, through intermediaries such as carriers, freight forwarders or other persons nominated by the seller or the buyer for a specific purpose.

The text of the Incoterms® 2010 rules is meant to be self-explanatory. However, in order to assist users the following text sets out guidance as to the sense in which selected terms are used throughout the document.

Carrier: For the purposes of the Incoterms® 2010 rules, the carrier is the party with whom carriage is contracted.

Customs formalities: These are requirements to be met in order to comply with any applicable customs regulations and may include documentary, security, information or physical inspection obligations.

Delivery: This concept has multiple meanings in trade law and practice, but in the Incoterms® 2010 rules, it is used to indicate where the risk of loss of or damage to the goods passes from the seller to the buyer.

Delivery document: This phrase is now used as the heading to article A8. It means a document used to prove that delivery has occurred. For many of the Incoterms® 2010 rules, the delivery document is a transport document or corresponding electronic record. However, with EXW, FCA, FAS and FOB, the delivery document may simply be a receipt. A delivery document may also have other functions, for example as part of the mechanism for payment.

Electronic record or procedure: A set of information constituted of one or more electronic messages and, where applicable, being functionally equivalent with the corresponding paper document.

Packaging: This word is used for different purposes:

1. The packaging of the goods to comply with any requirements under the contract of sale.

2. The packaging of the goods so that they are fit for transportation.

3. The stowage of the packaged goods within a container or other means of transport.

In the Incoterms® 2010 rules, packaging means both the first and second of the above. The Incoterms® 2010 rules do not deal with the parties' obligations for stowage within a container and therefore, where relevant, the parties should deal with this in the sale contract.

RULES FOR ANY MODE OR MODES OF TRANSPORT

EX WORKS

EXW (insert named place of delivery) Incoterms® 2010

GUIDANCE NOTE

This rule may be used irrespective of the mode of transport selected and may also be used where more than one mode of transport is employed. It is suitable for domestic trade, while FCA is usually more appropriate for international trade.

"Ex Works" means that the seller delivers when it places the goods at the disposal of the buyer at the seller's premises or at another named place (i.e., works, factory, warehouse, etc.). The seller does not need to load the goods on any collecting vehicle, nor does it need to clear the goods for export, where such clearance is applicable.

The parties are well advised to specify as clearly as possible the point within the named place of delivery, as the costs and risks to that point are for the account of the seller. The buyer bears all costs and risks involved in taking the goods from the agreed point, if any, at the named place of delivery.

EXW represents the minimum obligation for the seller. The rule should be used with care as:

a) The seller has no obligation to the buyer to load the goods, even though in practice the seller may be in a better position to do so. If the seller does load the goods, it does so at the buyer's risk and expense. In cases where the seller is in a better position to load the goods, FCA, which obliges the seller to do so at its own risk and expense, is usually more appropriate.

b) A buyer who buys from a seller on an EXW basis for export needs to be aware that the seller has an obligation to provide only such assistance as the buyer may require to effect that export: the seller is not bound to organize the export clearance. Buyers are therefore well advised not to use EXW if they cannot directly or indirectly obtain export clearance.

c) The buyer has limited obligations to provide to the seller any information regarding the export of the goods. However, the seller may need this information for, e.g., taxation or reporting purposes.

A THE SELLER'S OBLIGATIONS

A1 General obligations of the seller

The seller must provide the goods and the commercial invoice in conformity with the contract of sale and any other evidence of conformity that may be required by the contract.

Any document referred to in A1-A10 may be an equivalent electronic record or procedure if agreed between the parties or customary.

A2 Licences, authorizations, security clearances and other formalities

Where applicable, the seller must provide the buyer, at the buyer's request, risk and expense, assistance in obtaining any export licence, or other official authorization necessary for the export of the goods.

Where applicable, the seller must provide, at the buyer's request, risk and expense, any information in the possession of the seller that is required for the security clearance of the goods.

A3 Contracts of carriage and insurance

a) Contract of carriage
The seller has no obligation to the buyer to make a contract of carriage.

b) Contract of insurance
The seller has no obligation to the buyer to make a contract of insurance. However, the seller must provide the buyer, at the buyer's request, risk and expense (if any), with information that the buyer needs for obtaining insurance.

A4 Delivery

The seller must deliver the goods by placing them at the disposal of the buyer at the agreed point, if any, at the named place of delivery, not loaded on any collecting vehicle. If no specific point has been agreed within the named place of delivery, and if there are several points available, the seller may select the point that best suits its purpose. The seller must deliver the goods on the agreed date or within the agreed period.

B THE BUYER'S OBLIGATIONS

B1 General obligations of the buyer

The buyer must pay the price of the goods as provided in the contract of sale.

Any document referred to in B1-B10 may be an equivalent electronic record or procedure if agreed between the parties or customary.

B2 Licences, authorizations, security clearances and other formalities

Where applicable, it is up to the buyer to obtain, at its own risk and expense, any export and import licence or other official authorization and carry out all customs formalities for the export of the goods.

B3 Contracts of carriage and insurance

a) Contract of carriage
The buyer has no obligation to the seller to make a contract of carriage.

b) Contract of insurance
The buyer has no obligation to the seller to make a contract of insurance.

B4 Taking delivery

The buyer must take delivery of the goods when A4 and A7 have been complied with.

A5 Transfer of risks

The seller bears all risks of loss of or damage to the goods until they have been delivered in accordance with A4 with the exception of loss or damage in the circumstances described in B5.

A6 Allocation of costs

The seller must pay all costs relating to the goods until they have been delivered in accordance with A4, other than those payable by the buyer as envisaged in B6.

A7 Notices to the buyer

The seller must give the buyer any notice needed to enable the buyer to take delivery of the goods.

A8 Delivery document

The seller has no obligation to the buyer.

B5 **Transfer of risks**

The buyer bears all risks of loss of or damage to the goods from the time they have been delivered as envisaged in A4.

If the buyer fails to give notice in accordance with B7, then the buyer bears all risks of loss of or damage to the goods from the agreed date or the expiry date of the agreed period for delivery, provided that the goods have been clearly identified as the contract goods.

B6 **Allocation of costs**

The buyer must:

a) pay all costs relating to the goods from the time they have been delivered as envisaged in A4;

b) pay any additional costs incurred by failing either to take delivery of the goods when they have been placed at its disposal or to give appropriate notice in accordance with B7, provided that the goods have been clearly identified as the contract goods;

c) pay, where applicable, all duties, taxes and other charges, as well as the costs of carrying out customs formalities payable upon export; and

d) reimburse all costs and charges incurred by the seller in providing assistance as envisaged in A2.

B7 **Notices to the seller**

The buyer must, whenever it is entitled to determine the time within an agreed period and/or the point of taking delivery within the named place, give the seller sufficient notice thereof.

B8 **Proof of delivery**

The buyer must provide the seller with appropriate evidence of having taken delivery.

A9 **Checking – packaging – marking**

The seller must pay the costs of those checking operations (such as checking quality, measuring, weighing, counting) that are necessary for the purpose of delivering the goods in accordance with A4.

The seller must, at its own expense, package the goods, unless it is usual for the particular trade to transport the type of goods sold unpackaged. The seller may package the goods in the manner appropriate for their transport, unless the buyer has notified the seller of specific packaging requirements before the contract of sale is concluded. Packaging is to be marked appropriately.

A10 **Assistance with information and related costs**

The seller must, where applicable, in a timely manner, provide to or render assistance in obtaining for the buyer, at the buyer's request, risk and expense, any documents and information, including security-related information, that the buyer needs for the export and/or import of the goods and/or for their transport to the final destination.

B9 **Inspection of goods**

The buyer must pay the costs of any mandatory pre-shipment inspection, including inspection mandated by the authorities of the country of export.

B10 **Assistance with information and related costs**

The buyer must, in a timely manner, advise the seller of any security information requirements so that the seller may comply with A10.

The buyer must reimburse the seller for all costs and charges incurred by the seller in providing or rendering assistance in obtaining documents and information as envisaged in A10.

FCA

Free Carrier

FCA (insert named place of delivery) Incoterms® 2010

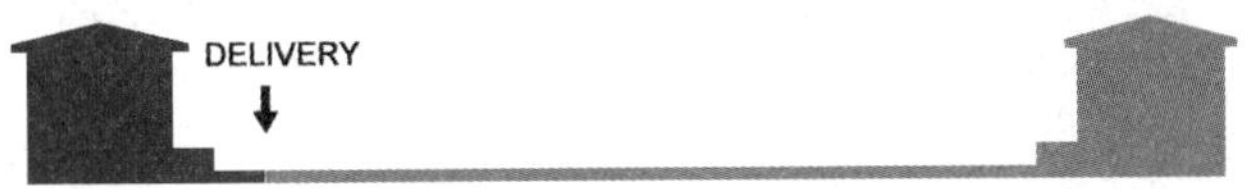

GUIDANCE NOTE

This rule may be used irrespective of the mode of transport selected and may also be used where more than one mode of transport is employed.

"Free Carrier" means that the seller delivers the goods to the carrier or another person nominated by the buyer at the seller's premises or another named place. The parties are well advised to specify as clearly as possible the point within the named place of delivery, as the risk passes to the buyer at that point.

If the parties intend to deliver the goods at the seller's premises, they should identify the address of those premises as the named place of delivery. If, on the other hand, the parties intend the goods to be delivered at another place, they must identify a different specific place of delivery.

FCA requires the seller to clear the goods for export, where applicable. However, the seller has no obligation to clear the goods for import, pay any import duty or carry out any import customs formalities.

A THE SELLER'S OBLIGATIONS

A1 General obligations of the seller

The seller must provide the goods and the commercial invoice in conformity with the contract of sale and any other evidence of conformity that may be required by the contract.

Any document referred to in A1-A10 may be an equivalent electronic record or procedure if agreed between the parties or customary.

A2 Licences, authorizations, security clearances and other formalities

Where applicable, the seller must obtain, at its own risk and expense, any export licence or other official authorization and carry out all customs formalities necessary for the export of the goods.

A3 Contracts of carriage and insurance

a) Contract of carriage
The seller has no obligation to the buyer to make a contract of carriage. However, if requested by the buyer or if it is commercial practice and the buyer does not give an instruction to the contrary in due time, the seller may contract for carriage on usual terms at the buyer's risk and expense. In either case, the seller may decline to make the contract of carriage and, if it does, shall promptly notify the buyer.

b) Contract of insurance
The seller has no obligation to the buyer to make a contract of insurance. However, the seller must provide the buyer, at the buyer's request, risk, and expense (if any), with information that the buyer needs for obtaining insurance.

A4 Delivery

The seller must deliver the goods to the carrier or another person nominated by the buyer at the agreed point, if any, at the named place on the agreed date or within the agreed period.

Delivery is completed:

a) If the named place is the seller's premises, when the goods have been loaded on the means of transport provided by the buyer.

b) In any other case, when the goods are placed at the disposal of the carrier or another person nominated by the buyer on the seller's means of transport ready for unloading.

B THE BUYER'S OBLIGATIONS

B1 General obligations of the buyer

The buyer must pay the price of the goods as provided in the contract of sale.

Any document referred to in B1-B10 may be an equivalent electronic record or procedure if agreed between the parties or customary.

B2 Licences, authorizations, security clearances and other formalities

Where applicable, it is up to the buyer to obtain, at its own risk and expense, any import licence or other official authorization and carry out all customs formalities for the import of the goods and for their transport through any country.

B3 Contracts of carriage and insurance

a) Contract of carriage
The buyer must contract at its own expense for the carriage of the goods from the named place of delivery, except when the contract of carriage is made by the seller as provided for in A3 a).

b) Contract of insurance
The buyer has no obligation to the seller to make a contract of insurance.

B4 Taking delivery

The buyer must take delivery of the goods when they have been delivered as envisaged in A4.

If no specific point has been notified by the buyer under B7 d) within the named place of delivery, and if there are several points available, the seller may select the point that best suits its purpose.

Unless the buyer notifies the seller otherwise, the seller may deliver the goods for carriage in such a manner as the quantity and/or nature of the goods may require.

A5 **Transfer of risks**

The seller bears all risks of loss of or damage to the goods until they have been delivered in accordance with A4, with the exception of loss or damage in the circumstances described in B5.

A6 **Allocation of costs**

The seller must pay

a) all costs relating to the goods until they have been delivered in accordance with A4, other than those payable by the buyer as envisaged in B6; and

b) where applicable, the costs of customs formalities necessary for export, as well as all duties, taxes, and other charges payable upon export.

B5 Transfer of risks

The buyer bears all risks of loss of or damage to the goods from the time they have been delivered as envisaged in A4.

If

a) the buyer fails in accordance with B7 to notify the nomination of a carrier or another person as envisaged in A4 or to give notice; or

b) the carrier or person nominated by the buyer as envisaged in A4 fails to take the goods into its charge,

then, the buyer bears all risks of loss of or damage to the goods:

(i) from the agreed date, or in the absence of an agreed date,

(ii) from the date notified by the seller under A7 within the agreed period; or, if no such date has been notified,

(iii) from the expiry date of any agreed period for delivery,

provided that the goods have been clearly identified as the contract goods.

B6 Allocation of costs

The buyer must pay

a) all costs relating to the goods from the time they have been delivered as envisaged in A4, except, where applicable, the costs of customs formalities necessary for export, as well as all duties, taxes, and other charges payable upon export as referred to in A6 b);

b) any additional costs incurred, either because:

(i) the buyer fails to nominate a carrier or another person as envisaged in A4, or

(ii) the carrier or person nominated by the buyer as envisaged in A4 fails to take the goods into its charge, or

(iii) the buyer has failed to give appropriate notice in accordance with B7,

provided that the goods have been clearly identified as the contract goods; and

A7 Notices to the buyer

The seller must, at the buyer's risk and expense, give the buyer sufficient notice either that the goods have been delivered in accordance with A4 or that the carrier or another person nominated by the buyer has failed to take the goods within the time agreed.

A8 Delivery document

The seller must provide the buyer, at the seller's expense, with the usual proof that the goods have been delivered in accordance with A4.

The seller must provide assistance to the buyer, at the buyer's request, risk and expense, in obtaining a transport document.

A9 Checking – packaging – marking

The seller must pay the costs of those checking operations (such as checking quality, measuring, weighing, counting) that are necessary for the purpose of delivering the goods in accordance with A4, as well as the costs of any pre-shipment inspection mandated by the authority of the country of export.

The seller must, at its own expense, package the goods, unless it is usual for the particular trade to transport the type of goods sold unpackaged. The seller may package the goods in the manner appropriate for their transport, unless the buyer has notified the seller of specific packaging requirements before the contract of sale is concluded. Packaging is to be marked appropriately.

c) where applicable, all duties, taxes and other charges as well as the costs of carrying out customs formalities payable upon import of the goods and the costs for their transport through any country.

B7 **Notices to the seller**

The buyer must notify the seller of

a) the name of the carrier or another person nominated as envisaged in A4 within sufficient time as to enable the seller to deliver the goods in accordance with that article;

b) where necessary, the selected time within the period agreed for delivery when the carrier or person nominated will take the goods;

c) the mode of transport to be used by the person nominated; and

d) the point of taking delivery within the named place.

B8 **Proof of delivery**

The buyer must accept the proof of delivery provided as envisaged in A8.

B9 **Inspection of goods**

The buyer must pay the costs of any mandatory pre-shipment inspection, except when such inspection is mandated by the authorities of the country of export.

A10 Assistance with information and related costs

The seller must, where applicable, in a timely manner, provide to or render assistance in obtaining for the buyer, at the buyer's request, risk and expense, any documents and information, including security-related information, that the buyer needs for the import of the goods and/or for their transport to the final destination.

The seller must reimburse the buyer for all costs and charges incurred by the buyer in providing or rendering assistance in obtaining documents and information as envisaged in B10.

B10 **Assistance with information and related costs**

The buyer must, in a timely manner, advise the seller of any security information requirements so that the seller may comply with A10.

The buyer must reimburse the seller for all costs and charges incurred by the seller in providing or rendering assistance in obtaining documents and information as envisaged in A10.

The buyer must, where applicable, in a timely manner, provide to or render assistance in obtaining for the seller, at the seller's request, risk and expense, any documents and information, including security-related information, that the seller needs for the transport and export of the goods and for their transport through any country.

CPT

CARRIAGE PAID TO

CPT (insert named place of destination) Incoterms® 2010

GUIDANCE NOTE

This rule may be used irrespective of the mode of transport selected and may also be used where more than one mode of transport is employed.

"Carriage Paid to" means that the seller delivers the goods to the carrier or another person nominated by the seller at an agreed place (if any such place is agreed between the parties) and that the seller must contract for and pay the costs of carriage necessary to bring the goods to the named place of destination.

When CPT, CIP, CFR or CIF are used, the seller fulfils its obligation to deliver when it hands the goods over to the carrier and not when the goods reach the place of destination.

This rule has two critical points, because risk passes and costs are transferred at different places. The parties are well advised to identify as precisely as possible in the contract both the place of delivery, where the risk passes to the buyer, and the named place of destination to which the seller must contract for the carriage. If several carriers are used for the carriage to the agreed destination and the parties do not agree on a specific point of delivery, the default position is that risk passes when the goods have been delivered to the first carrier at a point entirely of the seller's choosing and over which the buyer has no control. Should the parties wish the risk to pass at a later stage (e.g., at an ocean port or airport), they need to specify this in their contract of sale.

The parties are also well advised to identify as precisely as possible the point within the agreed place of destination, as the costs to that point are for the account of the seller. The seller is advised to procure contracts of carriage that match this choice precisely. If the seller incurs costs under its contract of carriage related to unloading at the named place of destination, the seller is not entitled to recover such costs from the buyer unless otherwise agreed between the parties.

CPT requires the seller to clear the goods for export, where applicable. However, the seller has no obligation to clear the goods for import, pay any import duty or carry out any import customs formalities.

A THE SELLER'S OBLIGATIONS

A1 General obligations of the seller

The seller must provide the goods and the commercial invoice in conformity with the contract of sale and any other evidence of conformity that may be required by the contract.

Any document referred to in A1-A10 may be an equivalent electronic record or procedure if agreed between the parties or customary.

A2 Licences, authorizations, security clearances and other formalities

Where applicable, the seller must obtain, at its own risk and expense, any export licence or other official authorization and carry out all customs formalities necessary for the export of the goods, and for their transport through any country prior to delivery.

A3 Contracts of carriage and insurance

a) Contract of carriage

The seller must contract or procure a contract for the carriage of the goods from the agreed point of delivery, if any, at the place of delivery to the named place of destination or, if agreed, any point at that place. The contract of carriage must be made on usual terms at the seller's expense and provide for carriage by the usual route and in a customary manner. If a specific point is not agreed or is not determined by practice, the seller may select the point of delivery and the point at the named place of destination that best suit its purpose.

b) Contract of insurance

The seller has no obligation to the buyer to make a contract of insurance. However, the seller must provide the buyer, at the buyer's request, risk, and expense (if any), with information that the buyer needs for obtaining insurance.

A4 Delivery

The seller must deliver the goods by handing them over to the carrier contracted in accordance with A3 on the agreed date or within the agreed period.

B THE BUYER'S OBLIGATIONS

B1 General obligations of the buyer

The buyer must pay the price of the goods as provided in the contract of sale.

Any document referred to in B1-B10 may be an equivalent electronic record or procedure if agreed between the parties or customary.

B2 Licences, authorizations, security clearances and other formalities

Where applicable, it is up to the buyer to obtain, at its own risk and expense, any import licence or other official authorization and carry out all customs formalities for the import of the goods and for their transport through any country.

B3 Contracts of carriage and insurance

a) Contract of carriage
The buyer has no obligation to the seller to make a contract of carriage.

b) Contract of insurance
The buyer has no obligation to the seller to make a contract of insurance. However, the buyer must provide the seller, upon request, with the necessary information for obtaining insurance.

B4 Taking delivery

The buyer must take delivery of the goods when they have been delivered as envisaged in A4 and receive them from the carrier at the named place of destination.

A5 Transfer of risks

The seller bears all risks of loss of or damage to the goods until they have been delivered in accordance with A4, with the exception of loss or damage in the circumstances described in B5.

A6 Allocation of costs

The seller must pay
a) all costs relating to the goods until they have been delivered in accordance with A4, other than those payable by the buyer as envisaged in B6;

b) the freight and all other costs resulting from A3 a), including the costs of loading the goods and any charges for unloading at the place of destination that were for the seller's account under the contract of carriage; and

c) where applicable, the costs of customs formalities necessary for export, as well as all duties, taxes and other charges payable upon export, and the costs for their transport through any country that were for the seller's account under the contract of carriage.

A7 Notices to the buyer

The seller must notify the buyer that the goods have been delivered in accordance with A4.

The seller must give the buyer any notice needed in order to allow the buyer to take measures that are normally necessary to enable the buyer to take the goods.

B5 **Transfer of risks**

The buyer bears all risks of loss of or damage to the goods from the time they have been delivered as envisaged in A4.

If the buyer fails to give notice in accordance with B7, it must bear all risks of loss of or damage to the goods from the agreed date or the expiry date of the agreed period for delivery, provided that the goods have been clearly identified as the contract goods.

B6 **Allocation of costs**

The buyer must, subject to the provisions of A3 a), pay
a) all costs relating to the goods from the time they have been delivered as envisaged in A4, except, where applicable, the costs of customs formalities necessary for export, as well as all duties, taxes, and other charges payable upon export as referred to in A6 c);

b) all costs and charges relating to the goods while in transit until their arrival at the agreed place of destination, unless such costs and charges were for the seller's account under the contract of carriage;

c) unloading costs, unless such costs were for the seller's account under the contract of carriage;

d) any additional costs incurred if the buyer fails to give notice in accordance with B7, from the agreed date or the expiry date of the agreed period for dispatch, provided that the goods have been clearly identified as the contract goods; and

e) where applicable, all duties, taxes and other charges, as well as the costs of carrying out customs formalities payable upon import of the goods and the costs for their transport through any country, unless included within the cost of the contract of carriage.

B7 **Notices to the seller**

The buyer must, whenever it is entitled to determine the time for dispatching the goods and/or the named place of destination or the point of receiving the goods within that place, give the seller sufficient notice thereof.

A8 Delivery document

If customary or at the buyer's request, the seller must provide the buyer, at the seller's expense, with the usual transport document[s] for the transport contracted in accordance with A3.

This transport document must cover the contract goods and be dated within the period agreed for shipment. If agreed or customary, the document must also enable the buyer to claim the goods from the carrier at the named place of destination and enable the buyer to sell the goods in transit by the transfer of the document to a subsequent buyer or by notification to the carrier.

When such a transport document is issued in negotiable form and in several originals, a full set of originals must be presented to the buyer.

A9 Checking – packaging – marking

The seller must pay the costs of those checking operations (such as checking quality, measuring, weighing, counting) that are necessary for the purpose of delivering the goods in accordance with A4, as well as the costs of any pre-shipment inspection mandated by the authority of the country of export.

The seller must, at its own expense, package the goods, unless it is usual for the particular trade to transport the type of goods sold unpackaged. The seller may package the goods in the manner appropriate for their transport, unless the buyer has notified the seller of specific packaging requirements before the contract of sale is concluded. Packaging is to be marked appropriately.

A10 Assistance with information and related costs

The seller must, where applicable, in a timely manner, provide to or render assistance in obtaining for the buyer, at the buyer's request, risk and expense, any documents and information, including security-related information, that the buyer needs for the import of the goods and/or for their transport to the final destination.

The seller must reimburse the buyer for all costs and charges incurred by the buyer in providing or rendering assistance in obtaining documents and information as envisaged in B10.

B8 **Proof of delivery**

The buyer must accept the transport document provided as envisaged in A8 if it is in conformity with the contract.

B9 **Inspection of goods**

The buyer must pay the costs of any mandatory pre-shipment inspection, except when such inspection is mandated by the authorities of the country of export.

B10 **Assistance with information and related costs**

The buyer must, in a timely manner, advise the seller of any security information requirements so that the seller may comply with A10.

The buyer must reimburse the seller for all costs and charges incurred by the seller in providing or rendering assistance in obtaining documents and information as envisaged in A10.

The buyer must, where applicable, in a timely manner, provide to or render assistance in obtaining for the seller, at the seller's request, risk and expense, any documents and information, including security-related information, that the seller needs for the transport and export of the goods and for their transport through any country.

CIP

CARRIAGE AND INSURANCE PAID TO

CIP (insert named place of destination) Incoterms® 2010

CIP

GUIDANCE NOTE

This rule may be used irrespective of the mode of transport selected and may also be used where more than one mode of transport is employed.

"Carriage and Insurance Paid to" means that the seller delivers the goods to the carrier or another person nominated by the seller at an agreed place (if any such place is agreed between the parties) and that the seller must contract for and pay the costs of carriage necessary to bring the goods to the named place of destination.

The seller also contracts for insurance cover against the buyer's risk of loss of or damage to the goods during the carriage. The buyer should note that under CIP the seller is required to obtain insurance only on minimum cover. Should the buyer wish to have more insurance protection, it will need either to agree as much expressly with the seller or to make its own extra insurance arrangements.

When CPT, CIP, CFR or CIF are used, the seller fulfils its obligation to deliver when it hands the goods over to the carrier and not when the goods reach the place of destination.

This rule has two critical points, because risk passes and costs are transferred at different places. The parties are well advised to identify as precisely as possible in the contract both the place of delivery, where the risk passes to the buyer, and the named place of destination to which the seller must contract for carriage. If several carriers are used for the carriage to the agreed destination and the parties do not agree on a specific point of delivery, the default position is that risk passes when the goods have been delivered to the first carrier at a point entirely of the seller's choosing and over which the buyer has no control. Should the parties wish the risk to pass at a later stage (e.g., at an ocean port or an airport), they need to specify this in their contract of sale.

The parties are also well advised to identify as precisely as possible the point within the agreed place of destination, as the costs to that point are for the account of the seller. The seller is advised to procure contracts of carriage that match this choice precisely. If the seller incurs costs under its contract of carriage related to unloading at the named place of destination, the seller is not entitled to recover such costs from the buyer unless otherwise agreed between the parties.

CIP requires the seller to clear the goods for export, where applicable. However, the seller has no obligation to clear the goods for import, pay any import duty or carry out any import customs formalities.

A THE SELLER'S OBLIGATIONS

A1 General obligations of the seller

The seller must provide the goods and the commercial invoice in conformity with the contract of sale and any other evidence of conformity that may be required by the contract.

Any document referred to in A1-A10 may be an equivalent electronic record or procedure if agreed between the parties or customary.

A2 Licences, authorizations, security clearances and other formalities

Where applicable, the seller must obtain, at its own risk and expense, any export licence or other official authorization and carry out all customs formalities necessary for the export of the goods and for their transport through any country prior to delivery.

B THE BUYER'S OBLIGATIONS

B1 General obligations of the buyer

The buyer must pay the price of the goods as provided in the contract of sale.

Any document referred to in B1-B10 may be an equivalent electronic record or procedure if agreed between the parties or customary.

B2 Licences, authorizations, security clearances and other formalities

Where applicable, it is up to the buyer to obtain, at its own risk and expense, any import licence or other official authorization and carry out all customs formalities for the import of the goods and for their transport through any country.

A3 **Contracts of carriage and insurance**

a) Contract of carriage

The seller must contract or procure a contract for the carriage of the goods from the agreed point of delivery, if any, at the place of delivery to the named place of destination or, if agreed, any point at that place. The contract of carriage must be made on usual terms at the seller's expense and provide for carriage by the usual route and in a customary manner. If a specific point is not agreed or is not determined by practice, the seller may select the point of delivery and the point at the named place of destination that best suit its purpose.

b) Contract of insurance

The seller must obtain at its own expense cargo insurance complying at least with the minimum cover as provided by Clauses (C) of the Institute Cargo Clauses (LMA/IUA) or any similar clauses. The insurance shall be contracted with underwriters or an insurance company of good repute and entitle the buyer, or any other person having an insurable interest in the goods, to claim directly from the insurer.

When required by the buyer, the seller shall, subject to the buyer providing any necessary information requested by the seller, provide at the buyer's expense any additional cover, if procurable, such as cover as provided by Clauses (A) or (B) of the Institute Cargo Clauses (LMA/IUA) or any similar clauses, and/or cover complying with the Institute War Clauses and/or Institute Strikes Clauses (LMA/IUA) or any similar clauses.

The insurance shall cover, at a minimum, the price provided in the contract plus 10% (i.e., 110%) and shall be in the currency of the contract.

The insurance shall cover the goods from the point of delivery set out in A4 and A5 to at least the named place of destination.

The seller must provide the buyer with the insurance policy or other evidence of insurance cover.

Moreover, the seller must provide the buyer, at the buyer's request, risk, and expense (if any), with information that the buyer needs to procure any additional insurance.

A4 **Delivery**

The seller must deliver the goods by handing them over to the carrier contracted in accordance with A3 on the agreed date or within the agreed period.

B3 **Contracts of carriage and insurance**

a) Contract of carriage

The buyer has no obligation to the seller to make a contract of carriage.

b) Contract of insurance

The buyer has no obligation to the seller to make a contract of insurance. However, the buyer must provide the seller, upon request, with any information necessary for the seller to procure any additional insurance requested by the buyer as envisaged in A3 b).

B4 **Taking delivery**

The buyer must take delivery of the goods when they have been delivered as envisaged in A4 and receive them from the carrier at the named place of destination.

A5 **Transfer of risks**

The seller bears all risks of loss of or damage to the goods until they have been delivered in accordance with A4, with the exception of loss or damage in the circumstances described in B5.

A6 **Allocation of costs**

The seller must pay

a) all costs relating to the goods until they have been delivered in accordance with A4, other than those payable by the buyer as envisaged in B6;

b) the freight and all other costs resulting from A3 a), including the costs of loading the goods and any charges for unloading at the place of destination that were for the seller's account under the contract of carriage;

c) the costs of insurance resulting from A3 b); and

d) where applicable, the costs of customs formalities necessary for export, as well as all duties, taxes and other charges payable upon export, and the costs for their transport through any country that were for the seller's account under the contract of carriage.

A7 **Notices to the buyer**

The seller must notify the buyer that the goods have been delivered in accordance with A4.

The seller must give the buyer any notice needed in order to allow the buyer to take measures that are normally necessary to enable the buyer to take the goods.

B5 **Transfer of risks**

The buyer bears all risks of loss of or damage to the goods from the time they have been delivered as envisaged in A4.

If the buyer fails to give notice in accordance with B7, it must bear all risks of loss of or damage to the goods from the agreed date or the expiry date of the agreed period for delivery, provided that the goods have been clearly identified as the contract goods.

B6 **Allocation of costs**

The buyer must, subject to the provisions of A3 a), pay
a) all costs relating to the goods from the time they have been delivered as envisaged in A4, except, where applicable, the costs of customs formalities necessary for export, as well as all duties, taxes and other charges payable upon export as referred to in A6 d);

b) all costs and charges relating to the goods while in transit until their arrival at the agreed place of destination, unless such costs and charges were for the seller's account under the contract of carriage;

c) unloading costs, unless such costs were for the seller's account under the contract of carriage;

d) any additional costs incurred if it fails to give notice in accordance with B7, from the agreed date or the expiry date of the agreed period for dispatch, provided that the goods have been clearly identified as the contract goods;

e) where applicable, all duties, taxes and other charges as well as the costs of carrying out customs formalities payable upon import of the goods and the costs for their transport through any country, unless included within the cost of the contract of carriage; and

f) the costs of any additional insurance procured at the buyer's request under A3 and B3.

B7 **Notices to the seller**

The buyer must, whenever it is entitled to determine the time for dispatching the goods and/or the named place of destination or the point of receiving the goods within that place, give the seller sufficient notice thereof.

A8 **Delivery document**

If customary or at the buyer's request, the seller must provide the buyer, at the seller's expense, with the usual transport document[s] for the transport contracted in accordance with A3.

This transport document must cover the contract goods and be dated within the period agreed for shipment. If agreed or customary, the document must also enable the buyer to claim the goods from the carrier at the named place of destination and enable the buyer to sell the goods in transit by the transfer of the document to a subsequent buyer or by notification to the carrier.

When such a transport document is issued in negotiable form and in several originals, a full set of originals must be presented to the buyer.

A9 **Checking – packaging – marking**

The seller must pay the costs of those checking operations (such as checking quality, measuring, weighing, counting) that are necessary for the purpose of delivering the goods in accordance with A4 as well as the costs of any pre-shipment inspection mandated by the authority of the country of export.

The seller must, at its own expense, package the goods, unless it is usual for the particular trade to transport the type of goods sold unpackaged. The seller may package the goods in the manner appropriate for their transport, unless the buyer has notified the seller of specific packaging requirements before the contract of sale is concluded. Packaging is to be marked appropriately.

A10 **Assistance with information and related costs**

The seller must, where applicable, in a timely manner, provide to or render assistance in obtaining for the buyer, at the buyer's request, risk and expense, any documents and information, including security-related information, that the buyer needs for the import of the goods and/or for their transport to the final destination.

The seller must reimburse the buyer for all costs and charges incurred by the buyer in providing or rendering assistance in obtaining documents and information as envisaged in B10.

B8 **Proof of delivery**

The buyer must accept the transport document provided as envisaged in A8 if it is in conformity with the contract.

B9 **Inspection of goods**

The buyer must pay the costs of any mandatory pre-shipment inspection, except when such inspection is mandated by the authorities of the country of export.

B10 **Assistance with information and related costs**

The buyer must, in a timely manner, advise the seller of any security information requirements so that the seller may comply with A10.

The buyer must reimburse the seller for all costs and charges incurred by the seller in providing or rendering assistance in obtaining documents and information as envisaged in A10.

The buyer must, where applicable, in a timely manner, provide to or render assistance in obtaining for the seller, at the seller's request, risk and expense, any documents and information, including security-related information, that the seller needs for the transport and export of the goods and for their transport through any country.

DAT

DELIVERED AT TERMINAL

DAT (insert named terminal at port or place of destination)
Incoterms® 2010

DAT

GUIDANCE NOTE

This rule may be used irrespective of the mode of transport selected and may also be used where more than one mode of transport is employed.

"Delivered at Terminal" means that the seller delivers when the goods, once unloaded from the arriving means of transport, are placed at the disposal of the buyer at a named terminal at the named port or place of destination. "Terminal" includes any place, whether covered or not, such as a quay, warehouse, container yard or road, rail or air cargo terminal. The seller bears all risks involved in bringing the goods to and unloading them at the terminal at the named port or place of destination.

The parties are well advised to specify as clearly as possible the terminal and, if possible, a specific point within the terminal at the agreed port or place of destination, as the risks to that point are for the account of the seller. The seller is advised to procure a contract of carriage that matches this choice precisely.

Moreover, if the parties intend the seller to bear the risks and costs involved in transporting and handling the goods from the terminal to another place, then the DAP or DDP rules should be used.

DAT requires the seller to clear the goods for export, where applicable. However, the seller has no obligation to clear the goods for import, pay any import duty or carry out any import customs formalities.

A THE SELLER'S OBLIGATIONS

A1 General obligations of the seller

The seller must provide the goods and the commercial invoice in conformity with the contract of sale and any other evidence of conformity that may be required by the contract.

Any document referred to in A1-A10 may be an equivalent electronic record or procedure if agreed between the parties or customary.

A2 Licences, authorizations, security clearances and other formalities

Where applicable, the seller must obtain, at its own risk and expense, any export licence and other official authorization and carry out all customs formalities necessary for the export of the goods and for their transport through any country prior to delivery.

A3 Contracts of carriage and insurance

a) Contract of carriage

The seller must contract at its own expense for the carriage of the goods to the named terminal at the agreed port or place of destination. If a specific terminal is not agreed or is not determined by practice, the seller may select the terminal at the agreed port or place of destination that best suits its purpose.

b) Contract of insurance

The seller has no obligation to the buyer to make a contract of insurance. However, the seller must provide the buyer, at the buyer's request, risk, and expense (if any), with information that the buyer needs for obtaining insurance.

A4 Delivery

The seller must unload the goods from the arriving means of transport and must then deliver them by placing them at the disposal of the buyer at the named terminal referred to in A3 a) at the port or place of destination on the agreed date or within the agreed period.

B THE BUYER'S OBLIGATIONS

B1 General obligations of the buyer

The buyer must pay the price of the goods as provided in the contract of sale.

Any document referred to in B1-B10 may be an equivalent electronic record or procedure if agreed between the parties or customary.

B2 Licences, authorizations, security clearances and other formalities

Where applicable, the buyer must obtain, at its own risk and expense, any import licence or other official authorization and carry out all customs formalities for the import of the goods.

B3 Contracts of carriage and insurance

a) Contract of carriage
The buyer has no obligation to the seller to make a contract of carriage.

b) Contract of insurance
The buyer has no obligation to the seller to make a contract of insurance. However, the buyer must provide the seller, upon request, with the necessary information for obtaining insurance.

B4 Taking delivery

The buyer must take delivery of the goods when they have been delivered as envisaged in A4.

A5 **Transfer of risks**

The seller bears all risks of loss of or damage to the goods until they have been delivered in accordance with A4 with the exception of loss or damage in the circumstances described in B5.

A6 **Allocation of costs**

The seller must pay

a) in addition to costs resulting from A3 a), all costs relating to the goods until they have been delivered in accordance with A4, other than those payable by the buyer as envisaged in B6; and

b) where applicable, the costs of customs formalities necessary for export as well as all duties, taxes and other charges payable upon export and the costs for their transport through any country, prior to delivery in accordance with A4.

A7 **Notices to the buyer**

The seller must give the buyer any notice needed in order to allow the buyer to take measures that are normally necessary to enable the buyer to take delivery of the goods.

A8 **Delivery document**

The seller must provide the buyer, at the seller's expense, with a document enabling the buyer to take delivery of the goods as envisaged in A4/B4.

B5 Transfer of risks

The buyer bears all risks of loss of or damage to the goods from the time they have been delivered as envisaged in A4.

If

a) the buyer fails to fulfil its obligations in accordance with B2, then it bears all resulting risks of loss of or damage to the goods; or

b) the buyer fails to give notice in accordance with B7, then it bears all risks of loss of or damage to the goods from the agreed date or the expiry date of the agreed period for delivery,

provided that the goods have been clearly identified as the contract goods.

B6 Allocation of costs

The buyer must pay

a) all costs relating to the goods from the time they have been delivered as envisaged in A4;

b) any additional costs incurred by the seller if the buyer fails to fulfil its obligations in accordance with B2, or to give notice in accordance with B7, provided that the goods have been clearly identified as the contract goods; and

c) where applicable, the costs of customs formalities as well as all duties, taxes and other charges payable upon import of the goods.

B7 Notices to the seller

The buyer must, whenever it is entitled to determine the time within an agreed period and/or the point of taking delivery at the named terminal, give the seller sufficient notice thereof.

B8 Proof of delivery

The buyer must accept the delivery document provided as envisaged in A8.

A9 Checking – packaging – marking

The seller must pay the costs of those checking operations (such as checking quality, measuring, weighing, counting) that are necessary for the purpose of delivering the goods in accordance with A4, as well as the costs of any pre-shipment inspection mandated by the authority of the country of export.

The seller must, at its own expense, package the goods, unless it is usual for the particular trade to transport the type of goods sold unpackaged. The seller may package the goods in the manner appropriate for their transport, unless the buyer has notified the seller of specific packaging requirements before the contract of sale is concluded. Packaging is to be marked appropriately.

A10 Assistance with information and related costs

The seller must, where applicable, in a timely manner, provide to or render assistance in obtaining for the buyer, at the buyer's request, risk and expense, any documents and information, including security-related information, that the buyer needs for the import of the goods and/or for their transport to the final destination.

The seller must reimburse the buyer for all costs and charges incurred by the buyer in providing or rendering assistance in obtaining documents and information as envisaged in B10.

B9 **Inspection of goods**

The buyer must pay the costs of any mandatory pre-shipment inspection, except when such inspection is mandated by the authorities of the country of export.

B10 **Assistance with information and related costs**

The buyer must, in a timely manner, advise the seller of any security information requirements so that the seller may comply with A10.

The buyer must reimburse the seller for all costs and charges incurred by the seller in providing or rendering assistance in obtaining documents and information as envisaged in A10.

The buyer must, where applicable, in a timely manner, provide to or render assistance in obtaining for the seller, at the seller's request, risk and expense, any documents and information, including security-related information, that the seller needs for the transport and export of the goods and for their transport through any country.

DAP

DELIVERED AT PLACE

DAP (insert named place of destination) Incoterms® 2010

DAP

GUIDANCE NOTE

This rule may be used irrespective of the mode of transport selected and may also be used where more than one mode of transport is employed.

"Delivered at Place" means that the seller delivers when the goods are placed at the disposal of the buyer on the arriving means of transport ready for unloading at the named place of destination. The seller bears all risks involved in bringing the goods to the named place.

The parties are well advised to specify as clearly as possible the point within the agreed place of destination, as the risks to that point are for the account of the seller. The seller is advised to procure contracts of carriage that match this choice precisely. If the seller incurs costs under its contract of carriage related to unloading at the place of destination, the seller is not entitled to recover such costs from the buyer unless otherwise agreed between the parties.

DAP requires the seller to clear the goods for export, where applicable. However, the seller has no obligation to clear the goods for import, pay any import duty or carry out any import customs formalities. If the parties wish the seller to clear the goods for import, pay any import duty and carry out any import customs formalities, the DDP term should be used.

A THE SELLER'S OBLIGATIONS

A1 General obligations of the seller

The seller must provide the goods and the commercial invoice in conformity with the contract of sale and any other evidence of conformity that may be required by the contract.

Any document referred to in A1-A10 may be an equivalent electronic record or procedure if agreed between the parties or customary.

A2 Licences, authorizations, security clearances and other formalities

Where applicable, the seller must obtain, at its own risk and expense, any export licence and other official authorization and carry out all customs formalities necessary for the export of the goods and for their transport through any country prior to delivery.

A3 Contracts of carriage and insurance

a) Contract of carriage
The seller must contract at its own expense for the carriage of the goods to the named place of destination or to the agreed point, if any, at the named place of destination. If a specific point is not agreed or is not determined by practice, the seller may select the point at the named place of destination that best suits its purpose.

b) Contract of insurance
The seller has no obligation to the buyer to make a contract of insurance. However, the seller must provide the buyer, at the buyer's request, risk, and expense (if any), with information that the buyer needs for obtaining insurance.

A4 Delivery

The seller must deliver the goods by placing them at the disposal of the buyer on the arriving means of transport ready for unloading at the agreed point, if any, at the named place of destination on the agreed date or within the agreed period.

B THE BUYER'S OBLIGATIONS

B1 General obligations of the buyer

The buyer must pay the price of the goods as provided in the contract of sale.

Any document referred to in B1-B10 may be an equivalent electronic record or procedure if agreed between the parties or customary.

B2 Licences, authorizations, security clearances and other formalities

Where applicable, the buyer must obtain, at its own risk and expense, any import licence or other official authorization and carry out all customs formalities for the import of the goods.

B3 Contracts of carriage and insurance

a) Contract of carriage
The buyer has no obligation to the seller to make a contract of carriage.

b) Contract of insurance
The buyer has no obligation to the seller to make a contract of insurance. However, the buyer must provide the seller, upon request, with the necessary information for obtaining insurance.

B4 Taking delivery

The buyer must take delivery of the goods when they have been delivered as envisaged in A4.

A5 **Transfer of risks**

The seller bears all risks of loss of or damage to the goods until they have been delivered in accordance with A4, with the exception of loss or damage in the circumstances described in B5.

A6 **Allocation of costs**

The seller must pay

a) in addition to costs resulting from A3 a), all costs relating to the goods until they have been delivered in accordance with A4, other than those payable by the buyer as envisaged in B6;

b) any charges for unloading at the place of destination that were for the seller's account under the contract of carriage; and

c) where applicable, the costs of customs formalities necessary for export as well as all duties, taxes and other charges payable upon export and the costs for their transport through any country, prior to delivery in accordance with A4.

A7 **Notices to the buyer**

The seller must give the buyer any notice needed in order to allow the buyer to take measures that are normally necessary to enable the buyer to take delivery of the goods.

B5 **Transfer of risks**

The buyer bears all risks of loss of or damage to the goods from the time they have been delivered as envisaged in A4.

If
a) the buyer fails to fulfil its obligations in accordance with B2, then it bears all resulting risks of loss of or damage to the goods; or

b) the buyer fails to give notice in accordance with B7, then it bears all risks of loss of or damage to the goods from the agreed date or the expiry date of the agreed period for delivery,

provided that the goods have been clearly identified as the contract goods.

B6 **Allocation of costs**

The buyer must pay
a) all costs relating to the goods from the time they have been delivered as envisaged in A4;

b) all costs of unloading necessary to take delivery of the goods from the arriving means of transport at the named place of destination, unless such costs were for the seller's account under the contract of carriage;

c) any additional costs incurred by the seller if the buyer fails to fulfil its obligations in accordance with B2 or to give notice in accordance with B7, provided that the goods have been clearly identified as the contract goods; and

d) where applicable, the costs of customs formalities, as well as all duties, taxes and other charges payable upon import of the goods.

B7 **Notices to the seller**

The buyer must, whenever it is entitled to determine the time within an agreed period and/or the point of taking delivery within the named place of destination, give the seller sufficient notice thereof.

A8 **Delivery document**

The seller must provide the buyer, at the seller's expense, with a document enabling the buyer to take delivery of the goods as envisaged in A4/B4.

A9 **Checking – packaging – marking**

The seller must pay the costs of those checking operations (such as checking quality, measuring, weighing, counting) that are necessary for the purpose of delivering the goods in accordance with A4, as well as the costs of any pre-shipment inspection mandated by the authority of the country of export.

The seller must, at its own expense, package the goods, unless it is usual for the particular trade to transport the type of goods sold unpackaged. The seller may package the goods in the manner appropriate for their transport, unless the buyer has notified the seller of specific packaging requirements before the contract of sale is concluded. Packaging is to be marked appropriately.

A10 **Assistance with information and related costs**

The seller must, where applicable, in a timely manner, provide to or render assistance in obtaining for the buyer, at the buyer's request, risk and expense, any documents and information, including security-related information, that the buyer needs for the import of the goods and/or for their transport to the final destination.

The seller must reimburse the buyer for all costs and charges incurred by the buyer in providing or rendering assistance in obtaining documents and information as envisaged in B10.

B8 Proof of delivery

The buyer must accept the delivery document provided as envisaged in A8.

B9 Inspection of goods

The buyer must pay the costs of any mandatory pre-shipment inspection, except when such inspection is mandated by the authorities of the country of export.

B10 Assistance with information and related costs

The buyer must, in a timely manner, advise the seller of any security information requirements so that the seller may comply with A10.

The buyer must reimburse the seller for all costs and charges incurred by the seller in providing or rendering assistance in obtaining documents and information as envisaged in A10.

The buyer must, where applicable, in a timely manner, provide to or render assistance in obtaining for the seller, at the seller's request, risk and expense, any documents and information, including security-related information, that the seller needs for the transport and export of the goods and for their transport through any country.

DDP

DELIVERED DUTY PAID

DDP (insert named place of destination) Incoterms® 2010

GUIDANCE NOTE

This rule may be used irrespective of the mode of transport selected and may also be used where more than one mode of transport is employed.

"Delivered Duty Paid" means that the seller delivers the goods when the goods are placed at the disposal of the buyer, cleared for import on the arriving means of transport ready for unloading at the named place of destination. The seller bears all the costs and risks involved in bringing the goods to the place of destination and has an obligation to clear the goods not only for export but also for import, to pay any duty for both export and import and to carry out all customs formalities.

DDP represents the maximum obligation for the seller.

The parties are well advised to specify as clearly as possible the point within the agreed place of destination, as the costs and risks to that point are for the account of the seller. The seller is advised to procure contracts of carriage that match this choice precisely. If the seller incurs costs under its contract of carriage related to unloading at the place of destination, the seller is not entitled to recover such costs from the buyer unless otherwise agreed between the parties.

The parties are well advised not to use DDP if the seller is unable directly or indirectly to obtain import clearance.

If the parties wish the buyer to bear all risks and costs of import clearance, the DAP rule should be used.

Any VAT or other taxes payable upon import are for the seller's account unless expressly agreed otherwise in the sale contract.

A THE SELLER'S OBLIGATIONS

A1 General obligations of the seller

The seller must provide the goods and the commercial invoice in conformity with the contract of sale and any other evidence of conformity that may be required by the contract.

Any document referred to in A1-A10 may be an equivalent electronic record or procedure if agreed between the parties or customary.

A2 Licences, authorizations, security clearances and other formalities

Where applicable, the seller must obtain, at its own risk and expense, any export and import licence and other official authorization and carry out all customs formalities necessary for the export of the goods, for their transport through any country and for their import.

A3 Contracts of carriage and insurance

a) Contract of carriage
The seller must contract at its own expense for the carriage of the goods to the named place of destination or to the agreed point, if any, at the named place of destination. If a specific point is not agreed or is not determined by practice, the seller may select the point at the named place of destination that best suits its purpose.

b) Contract of insurance
The seller has no obligation to the buyer to make a contract of insurance. However, the seller must provide the buyer, at the buyer's request, risk, and expense (if any), with information that the buyer needs for obtaining insurance.

A4 Delivery

The seller must deliver the goods by placing them at the disposal of the buyer on the arriving means of transport ready for unloading at the agreed point, if any, at the named place of destination on the agreed date or within the agreed period.

B THE BUYER'S OBLIGATIONS

B1 General obligations of the buyer

The buyer must pay the price of the goods as provided in the contract of sale.

Any document referred to in B1-B10 may be an equivalent electronic record or procedure if agreed between the parties or customary.

B2 Licences, authorizations, security clearances and other formalities

Where applicable, the buyer must provide assistance to the seller, at the seller's request, risk and expense, in obtaining any import licence or other official authorization for the import of the goods.

B3 Contracts of carriage and insurance

a) Contract of carriage
The buyer has no obligation to the seller to make a contract of carriage.

b) Contract of insurance
The buyer has no obligation to the seller to make a contract of insurance. However, the buyer must provide the seller, upon request, with the necessary information for obtaining insurance.

B4 Taking delivery

The buyer must take delivery of the goods when they have been delivered as envisaged in A4.

A5 **Transfer of risks**

The seller bears all risks of loss of or damage to the goods until they have been delivered in accordance with A4, with the exception of loss or damage in the circumstances described in B5.

A6 **Allocation of costs**

The seller must pay

a) in addition to costs resulting from A3 a), all costs relating to the goods until they have been delivered in accordance with A4, other than those payable by the buyer as envisaged in B6;

b) any charges for unloading at the place of destination that were for the seller's account under the contract of carriage; and

c) where applicable, the costs of customs formalities necessary for export and import as well as all duties, taxes and other charges payable upon export and import of the goods, and the costs for their transport through any country prior to delivery in accordance with A4.

A7 **Notices to the buyer**

The seller must give the buyer any notice needed in order to allow the buyer to take measures that are normally necessary to enable the buyer to take delivery of the goods.

A8 **Delivery document**

The seller must provide the buyer, at the seller's expense, with a document enabling the buyer to take delivery of the goods as envisaged in A4/B4.

B5 **Transfer of risks**

The buyer bears all risks of loss of or damage to the goods from the time they have been delivered as envisaged in A4.

If
a) the buyer fails to fulfil its obligations in accordance with B2, then it bears all resulting risks of loss of or damage to the goods; or

b) the buyer fails to give notice in accordance with B7, then it bears all risks of loss of or damage to the goods from the agreed date or the expiry date of the agreed period for delivery,

provided that the goods have been clearly identified as the contract goods.

B6 **Allocation of costs**

The buyer must pay
a) all costs relating to the goods from the time they have been delivered as envisaged in A4;

b) all costs of unloading necessary to take delivery of the goods from the arriving means of transport at the named place of destination, unless such costs were for the seller's account under the contract of carriage; and

c) any additional costs incurred if it fails to fulfil its obligations in accordance with B2 or to give notice in accordance with B7, provided that the goods have been clearly identified as the contract goods.

B7 **Notices to the seller**

The buyer must, whenever it is entitled to determine the time within an agreed period and/or the point of taking delivery within the named place of destination, give the seller sufficient notice thereof.

B8 **Proof of delivery**

The buyer must accept the proof of delivery provided as envisaged in A8.

A9 **Checking – packaging – marking**

The seller must pay the costs of those checking operations (such as checking quality, measuring, weighing, counting) that are necessary for the purpose of delivering the goods in accordance with A4, as well as the costs of any pre-shipment inspection mandated by the authority of the country of export or of import.

The seller must, at its own expense, package the goods, unless it is usual for the particular trade to transport the type of goods sold unpackaged. The seller may package the goods in the manner appropriate for their transport, unless the buyer has notified the seller of specific packaging requirements before the contract of sale is concluded. Packaging is to be marked appropriately.

A10 **Assistance with information and related costs**

The seller must, where applicable, in a timely manner, provide to or render assistance in obtaining for the buyer, at the buyer's request, risk and expense, any documents and information, including security-related information, that the buyer needs for the transport of the goods to the final destination, where applicable, from the named place of destination.

The seller must reimburse the buyer for all costs and charges incurred by the buyer in providing or rendering assistance in obtaining documents and information as envisaged in B10.

B9 **Inspection of goods**

The buyer has no obligation to the seller to pay the costs of any mandatory pre-shipment inspection mandated by the authority of the country of export or of import.

B10 **Assistance with information and related costs**

The buyer must, in a timely manner, advise the seller of any security information requirements so that the seller may comply with A10.

The buyer must reimburse the seller for all costs and charges incurred by the seller in providing or rendering assistance in obtaining documents and information as envisaged in A10.

The buyer must, where applicable, in a timely manner, provide to or render assistance in obtaining for the seller, at the seller's request, risk and expense, any documents and information, including security-related information, that the seller needs for the transport, export and import of the goods and for their transport through any country.

RULES FOR SEA AND INLAND WATERWAY TRANSPORT

FAS

FREE ALONGSIDE SHIP

FAS (insert named port of shipment) Incoterms® 2010

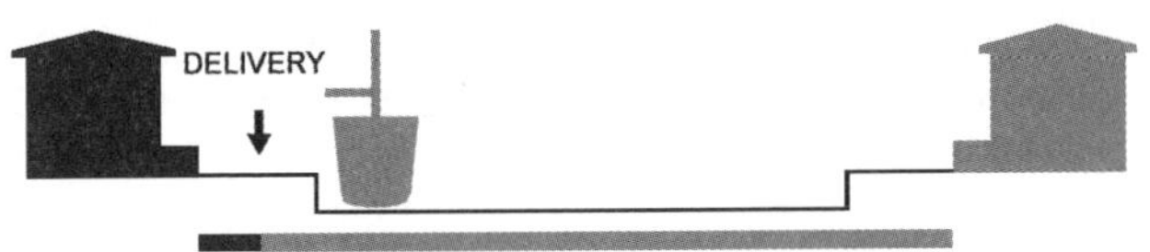

GUIDANCE NOTE

This rule is to be used only for sea or inland waterway transport.

"Free Alongside Ship" means that the seller delivers when the goods are placed alongside the vessel (e.g., on a quay or a barge) nominated by the buyer at the named port of shipment. The risk of loss of or damage to the goods passes when the goods are alongside the ship, and the buyer bears all costs from that moment onwards.

The parties are well advised to specify as clearly as possible the loading point at the named port of shipment, as the costs and risks to that point are for the account of the seller and these costs and associated handling charges may vary according to the practice of the port.

The seller is required either to deliver the goods alongside the ship or to procure goods already so delivered for shipment. The reference to "procure" here caters for multiple sales down a chain ('string sales'), particularly common in the commodity trades.

Where the goods are in containers, it is typical for the seller to hand the goods over to the carrier at a terminal and not alongside the vessel. In such situations, the FAS rule would be inappropriate, and the FCA rule should be used.

FAS requires the seller to clear the goods for export, where applicable. However, the seller has no obligation to clear the goods for import, pay any import duty or carry out any import customs formalities.

A THE SELLER'S OBLIGATIONS

A1 General obligations of the seller

The seller must provide the goods and the commercial invoice in conformity with the contract of sale and any other evidence of conformity that may be required by the contract.

Any document referred to in A1-A10 may be an equivalent electronic record or procedure if agreed between the parties or customary.

A2 Licences, authorizations, security clearances and other formalities

Where applicable, the seller must obtain, at its own risk and expense, any export licence or other official authorization and carry out all customs formalities necessary for the export of the goods.

A3 Contracts of carriage and insurance

a) Contract of carriage
The seller has no obligation to the buyer to make a contract of carriage. However, if requested by the buyer or if it is commercial practice and the buyer does not give an instruction to the contrary in due time, the seller may contract for carriage on usual terms at the buyer's risk and expense. In either case, the seller may decline to make the contract of carriage and, if it does, shall promptly notify the buyer.

b) Contract of insurance
The seller has no obligation to the buyer to make a contract of insurance. However, the seller must provide the buyer, at the buyer's request, risk, and expense (if any), with information that the buyer needs for obtaining insurance.

A4 Delivery

The seller must deliver the goods either by placing them alongside the ship nominated by the buyer at the loading point, if any, indicated by the buyer at the named port of shipment or by procuring the goods so delivered. In either case, the seller must deliver the goods on the agreed date or within the agreed period and in the manner customary at the port.

If no specific loading point has been indicated by the buyer, the seller may select the point within the named port of shipment that best suits its purpose. If the parties have agreed that delivery should take place within a period, the buyer has the option to choose the date within that period.

B THE BUYER'S OBLIGATIONS

B1 General obligations of the buyer

The buyer must pay the price of the goods as provided in the contract of sale.

Any document referred to in B1-B10 may be an equivalent electronic record or procedure if agreed between the parties or customary.

B2 Licences, authorizations, security clearances and other formalities

Where applicable, it is up to the buyer to obtain, at its own risk and expense, any import licence or other official authorization and carry out all customs formalities for the import of the goods and for their transport through any country.

B3 Contracts of carriage and insurance

a) Contract of carriage
The buyer must contract, at its own expense for the carriage of the goods from the named port of shipment, except where the contract of carriage is made by the seller as provided for in A3 a).

b) Contract of insurance
The buyer has no obligation to the seller to make a contract of insurance.

B4 Taking delivery

The buyer must take delivery of the goods when they have been delivered as envisaged in A4.

A5 **Transfer of risks**

The seller bears all risks of loss of or damage to the goods until they have been delivered in accordance with A4 with the exception of loss or damage in the circumstances described in B5.

A6 **Allocation of costs**

The seller must pay

a) all costs relating to the goods until they have been delivered in accordance with A4, other than those payable by the buyer as envisaged in B6; and

b) where applicable, the costs of customs formalities necessary for export as well as all duties, taxes and other charges payable upon export.

A7 **Notices to the buyer**

The seller must, at the buyer's risk and expense, give the buyer sufficient notice either that the goods have been delivered in accordance with A4 or that the vessel has failed to take the goods within the time agreed.

B5 **Transfer of risks**

The buyer bears all risks of loss of or damage to the goods from the time they have been delivered as envisaged in A4.

If
a) the buyer fails to give notice in accordance with B7; or

b) the vessel nominated by the buyer fails to arrive on time, or fails to take the goods or closes for cargo earlier than the time notified in accordance with B7;

then the buyer bears all risks of loss of or damage to the goods from the agreed date or the expiry date of the agreed period for delivery, provided that the goods have been clearly identified as the contract goods.

B6 **Allocation of costs**

The buyer must pay
a) all costs relating to the goods from the time they have been delivered as envisaged in A4, except, where applicable, the costs of customs formalities necessary for export as well as all duties, taxes, and other charges payable upon export as referred to in A6 b);

b) any additional costs incurred, either because:
(i) the buyer has failed to give appropriate notice in accordance with B7, or
(ii) the vessel nominated by the buyer fails to arrive on time, is unable to take the goods, or closes for cargo earlier than the time notified in accordance with B7,

provided that the goods have been clearly identified as the contract goods; and

c) where applicable, all duties, taxes and other charges, as well as the costs of carrying out customs formalities payable upon import of the goods and the costs for their transport through any country.

B7 **Notices to the seller**

The buyer must give the seller sufficient notice of the vessel name, loading point and, where necessary, the selected delivery time within the agreed period.

A8 Delivery document

The seller must provide the buyer, at the seller's expense, with the usual proof that the goods have been delivered in accordance with A4.

Unless such proof is a transport document, the seller must provide assistance to the buyer, at the buyer's request, risk and expense, in obtaining a transport document.

A9 Checking – packaging – marking

The seller must pay the costs of those checking operations (such as checking quality, measuring, weighing, counting) that are necessary for the purpose of delivering the goods in accordance with A4, as well as the costs of any pre-shipment inspection mandated by the authority of the country of export.

The seller must, at its own expense, package the goods, unless it is usual for the particular trade to transport the type of goods sold unpackaged. The seller may package the goods in the manner appropriate for their transport, unless the buyer has notified the seller of specific packaging requirements before the contract of sale is concluded. Packaging is to be marked appropriately.

A10 Assistance with information and related costs

The seller must, where applicable, in a timely manner, provide to or render assistance in obtaining for the buyer, at the buyer's request, risk and expense, any documents and information, including security-related information, that the buyer needs for the import of the goods and/or for their transport to the final destination.

The seller must reimburse the buyer for all costs and charges incurred by the buyer in providing or rendering assistance in obtaining documents and information as envisaged in B10.

B8 **Proof of delivery**

The buyer must accept the proof of delivery provided as envisaged in A8.

B9 **Inspection of goods**

The buyer must pay the costs of any mandatory pre-shipment inspection, except when such inspection is mandated by the authorities of the country of export.

B10 **Assistance with information and related costs**

The buyer must, in a timely manner, advise the seller of any security information requirements so that the seller may comply with A10.

The buyer must reimburse the seller for all costs and charges incurred by the seller in providing or rendering assistance in obtaining documents and information as envisaged in A10.

The buyer must, where applicable, in a timely manner, provide to or render assistance in obtaining for the seller, at the seller's request, risk and expense, any documents and information, including security-related information, that the seller needs for the transport and export of the goods and for their transport through any country.

FOB

FREE ON BOARD

FOB (insert named port of shipment) Incoterms® 2010

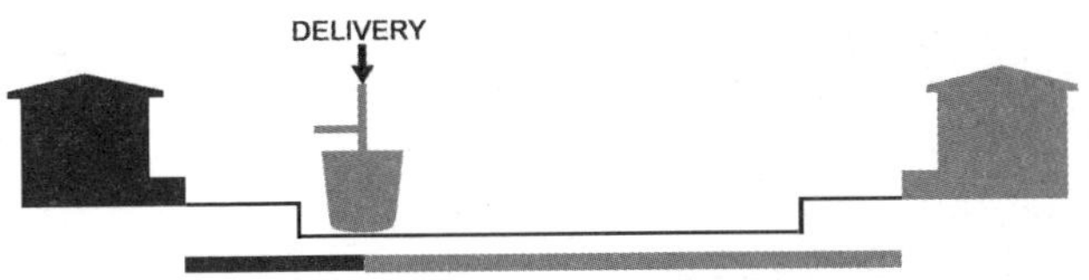

GUIDANCE NOTE

This rule is to be used only for sea or inland waterway transport.

"Free on Board" means that the seller delivers the goods on board the vessel nominated by the buyer at the named port of shipment or procures the goods already so delivered. The risk of loss of or damage to the goods passes when the goods are on board the vessel, and the buyer bears all costs from that moment onwards.

The seller is required either to deliver the goods on board the vessel or to procure goods already so delivered for shipment. The reference to "procure" here caters for multiple sales down a chain ('string sales'), particularly common in the commodity trades.

FOB may not be appropriate where goods are handed over to the carrier before they are on board the vessel, for example goods in containers, which are typically delivered at a terminal. In such situations, the FCA rule should be used.

FOB requires the seller to clear the goods for export, where applicable. However, the seller has no obligation to clear the goods for import, pay any import duty or carry out any import customs formalities.

A THE SELLER'S OBLIGATIONS

A1 General obligations of the seller

The seller must provide the goods and the commercial invoice in conformity with the contract of sale and any other evidence of conformity that may be required by the contract.

Any document referred to in A1-A10 may be an equivalent electronic record or procedure if agreed between the parties or customary.

A2 Licences, authorizations, security clearances and other formalities

Where applicable, the seller must obtain, at its own risk and expense, any export licence or other official authorization and carry out all customs formalities necessary for the export of the goods.

A3 Contracts of carriage and insurance

a) Contract of carriage
The seller has no obligation to the buyer to make a contract of carriage. However, if requested by the buyer or if it is commercial practice and the buyer does not give an instruction to the contrary in due time, the seller may contract for carriage on usual terms at the buyer's risk and expense. In either case, the seller may decline to make the contract of carriage and, if it does, shall promptly notify the buyer.

b) Contract of insurance
The seller has no obligation to the buyer to make a contract of insurance. However, the seller must provide the buyer, at the buyer's request, risk, and expense (if any), with information that the buyer needs for obtaining insurance.

A4 Delivery

The seller must deliver the goods either by placing them on board the vessel nominated by the buyer at the loading point, if any, indicated by the buyer at the named port of shipment or by procuring the goods so delivered. In either case, the seller must deliver the goods on the agreed date or within the agreed period and in the manner customary at the port.

If no specific loading point has been indicated by the buyer, the seller may select the point within the named port of shipment that best suits its purpose.

FOB

B THE BUYER'S OBLIGATIONS

B1 General obligations of the buyer

The buyer must pay the price of the goods as provided in the contract of sale.

Any document referred to in B1-B10 may be an equivalent electronic record or procedure if agreed between the parties or customary.

B2 Licences, authorizations, security clearances and other formalities

Where applicable, it is up to the buyer to obtain, at its own risk and expense, any import licence or other official authorization and carry out all customs formalities for the import of the goods and for their transport through any country.

B3 Contracts of carriage and insurance

a) Contract of carriage
The buyer must contract, at its own expense for the carriage of the goods from the named port of shipment, except where the contract of carriage is made by the seller as provided for in A3 a).

b) Contract of insurance
The buyer has no obligation to the seller to make a contract of insurance.

B4 Taking delivery

The buyer must take delivery of the goods when they have been delivered as envisaged in A4.

A5 **Transfer of risks**

The seller bears all risks of loss of or damage to the goods until they have been delivered in accordance with A4 with the exception of loss or damage in the circumstances described in B5.

A6 **Allocation of costs**

The seller must pay

a) all costs relating to the goods until they have been delivered in accordance with A4, other than those payable by the buyer as envisaged in B6; and

b) where applicable, the costs of customs formalities necessary for export, as well as all duties, taxes and other charges payable upon export.

B5 Transfer of risks

The buyer bears all risks of loss of or damage to the goods from the time they have been delivered as envisaged in A4.

If

a) the buyer fails to notify the nomination of a vessel in accordance with B7; or

b) the vessel nominated by the buyer fails to arrive on time to enable the seller to comply with A4, is unable to take the goods, or closes for cargo earlier than the time notified in accordance with B7;

then, the buyer bears all risks of loss of or damage to the goods:

(i) from the agreed date, or in the absence of an agreed date,

(ii) from the date notified by the seller under A7 within the agreed period, or, if no such date has been notified,

(iii) from the expiry date of any agreed period for delivery,

provided that the goods have been clearly identified as the contract goods.

B6 Allocation of costs

The buyer must pay

a) all costs relating to the goods from the time they have been delivered as envisaged in A4, except, where applicable, the costs of customs formalities necessary for export, as well as all duties, taxes and other charges payable upon export as referred to in A6 b);

b) any additional costs incurred, either because:

(i) the buyer has failed to give appropriate notice in accordance with B7, or

(ii) the vessel nominated by the buyer fails to arrive on time, is unable to take the goods, or closes for cargo earlier than the time notified in accordance with B7,

provided that the goods have been clearly identified as the contract goods; and

c) where applicable, all duties, taxes and other charges, as well as the costs of carrying out customs formalities payable upon import of the goods and the costs for their transport through any country.

A7 Notices to the buyer

The seller must, at the buyer's risk and expense, give the buyer sufficient notice either that the goods have been delivered in accordance with A4 or that the vessel has failed to take the goods within the time agreed.

A8 Delivery document

The seller must provide the buyer, at the seller's expense, with the usual proof that the goods have been delivered in accordance with A4.

Unless such proof is a transport document, the seller must provide assistance to the buyer, at the buyer's request, risk and expense, in obtaining a transport document.

A9 Checking – packaging – marking

The seller must pay the costs of those checking operations (such as checking quality, measuring, weighing, counting) that are necessary for the purpose of delivering the goods in accordance with A4, as well as the costs of any pre-shipment inspection mandated by the authority of the country of export.

The seller must, at its own expense, package the goods, unless it is usual for the particular trade to transport the type of goods sold unpackaged. The seller may package the goods in the manner appropriate for their transport, unless the buyer has notified the seller of specific packaging requirements before the contract of sale is concluded. Packaging is to be marked appropriately.

A10 Assistance with information and related costs

The seller must, where applicable, in a timely manner, provide to or render assistance in obtaining for the buyer, at the buyer's request, risk and expense, any documents and information, including security-related information, that the buyer needs for the import of the goods and/or for their transport to the final destination.

The seller must reimburse the buyer for all costs and charges incurred by the buyer in providing or rendering assistance in obtaining documents and information as envisaged in B10.

B7 **Notices to the seller**

The buyer must give the seller sufficient notice of the vessel name, loading point and, where necessary, the selected delivery time within the agreed period.

B8 **Proof of delivery**

The buyer must accept the proof of delivery provided as envisaged in A8.

B9 **Inspection of goods**

The buyer must pay the costs of any mandatory pre-shipment inspection, except when such inspection is mandated by the authorities of the country of export.

B10 **Assistance with information and related costs**

The buyer must, in a timely manner, advise the seller of any security information requirements so that the seller may comply with A10.

The buyer must reimburse the seller for all costs and charges incurred by the seller in providing or rendering assistance in obtaining documents and information as envisaged in A10.

The buyer must, where applicable, in a timely manner, provide to or render assistance in obtaining for the seller, at the seller's request, risk and expense, any documents and information, including security-related information, that the seller needs for the transport and export of the goods and for their transport through any country.

CFR

COST AND FREIGHT

CFR (insert named port of destination) Incoterms® 2010

GUIDANCE NOTE

This rule is to be used only for sea or inland waterway transport.

"Cost and Freight" means that the seller delivers the goods on board the vessel or procures the goods already so delivered. The risk of loss of or damage to the goods passes when the goods are on board the vessel. The seller must contract for and pay the costs and freight necessary to bring the goods to the named port of destination.

When CPT, CIP, CFR or CIF are used, the seller fulfils its obligation to deliver when it hands the goods over to the carrier in the manner specified in the chosen rule and not when the goods reach the place of destination.

This rule has two critical points, because risk passes and costs are transferred at different places. While the contract will always specify a destination port, it might not specify the port of shipment, which is where risk passes to the buyer. If the shipment port is of particular interest to the buyer, the parties are well advised to identify it as precisely as possible in the contract.

The parties are well advised to identify as precisely as possible the point at the agreed port of destination, as the costs to that point are for the account of the seller. The seller is advised to procure contracts of carriage that match this choice precisely. If the seller incurs costs under its contract of carriage related to unloading at the specified point at the port of destination, the seller is not entitled to recover such costs from the buyer unless otherwise agreed between the parties.

The seller is required either to deliver the goods on board the vessel or to procure goods already so delivered for shipment to the destination. In addition, the seller is required either to make a contract of carriage or to procure such a contract. The reference to "procure" here caters for multiple sales down a chain ('string sales'), particularly common in the commodity trades.

CFR may not be appropriate where goods are handed over to the carrier before they are on board the vessel, for example goods in containers, which are typically delivered at a terminal. In such circumstances, the CPT rule should be used.

CFR requires the seller to clear the goods for export, where applicable. However, the seller has no obligation to clear the goods for import, pay any import duty or carry out any import customs formalities.

A THE SELLER'S OBLIGATIONS

A1 General obligations of the seller

The seller must provide the goods and the commercial invoice in conformity with the contract of sale and any other evidence of conformity that may be required by the contract.

Any document referred to in A1-A10 may be an equivalent electronic record or procedure if agreed between the parties or customary.

A2 Licences, authorizations, security clearances and other formalities

Where applicable, the seller must obtain, at its own risk and expense, any export licence or other official authorization and carry out all customs formalities necessary for the export of the goods.

A3 Contracts of carriage and insurance

a) Contract of carriage
The seller must contract or procure a contract for the carriage of the goods from the agreed point of delivery, if any, at the place of delivery to the named port of destination or, if agreed, any point at that port. The contract of carriage must be made on usual terms at the seller's expense and provide for carriage by the usual route in a vessel of the type normally used for the transport of the type of goods sold.

b) Contract of insurance
The seller has no obligation to the buyer to make a contract of insurance. However, the seller must provide the buyer, at the buyer's request, risk, and expense (if any), with information that the buyer needs for obtaining insurance.

A4 Delivery

The seller must deliver the goods either by placing them on board the vessel or by procuring the goods so delivered. In either case, the seller must deliver the goods on the agreed date or within the agreed period and in the manner customary at the port.

B THE BUYER'S OBLIGATIONS

B1 General obligations of the buyer

The buyer must pay the price of the goods as provided in the contract of sale.

Any document referred to in B1-B10 may be an equivalent electronic record or procedure if agreed between the parties or customary.

B2 Licences, authorizations, security clearances and other formalities

Where applicable, it is up to the buyer to obtain, at its own risk and expense, any import licence or other official authorization and carry out all customs formalities for the import of the goods and for their transport through any country.

B3 Contracts of carriage and insurance

a) Contract of carriage

The buyer has no obligation to the seller to make a contract of carriage.

b) Contract of insurance

The buyer has no obligation to the seller to make a contract of insurance. However, the buyer must provide the seller, upon request, with the necessary information for obtaining insurance.

B4 Taking delivery

The buyer must take delivery of the goods when they have been delivered as envisaged in A4 and receive them from the carrier at the named port of destination.

A5 **Transfer of risks**

The seller bears all risks of loss of or damage to the goods until they have been delivered in accordance with A4, with the exception of loss or damage in the circumstances described in B5.

A6 **Allocation of costs**

The seller must pay

a) all costs relating to the goods until they have been delivered in accordance with A4, other than those payable by the buyer as envisaged in B6;

b) the freight and all other costs resulting from A3 a), including the costs of loading the goods on board and any charges for unloading at the agreed port of discharge that were for the seller's account under the contract of carriage; and

c) where applicable, the costs of customs formalities necessary for export as well as all duties, taxes and other charges payable upon export, and the costs for their transport through any country that were for the seller's account under the contract of carriage.

A7 **Notices to the buyer**

The seller must give the buyer any notice needed in order to allow the buyer to take measures that are normally necessary to enable the buyer to take the goods.

B5 Transfer of risks

The buyer bears all risks of loss of or damage to the goods from the time they have been delivered as envisaged in A4.

If the buyer fails to give notice in accordance with B7, then it bears all risks of loss of or damage to the goods from the agreed date or the expiry date of the agreed period for shipment, provided that the goods have been clearly identified as the contract goods.

B6 Allocation of costs

The buyer must, subject to the provisions of A3 a), pay
a) all costs relating to the goods from the time they have been delivered as envisaged in A4, except, where applicable, the costs of customs formalities necessary for export as well as all duties, taxes, and other charges payable upon export as referred to in A6 c);

b) all costs and charges relating to the goods while in transit until their arrival at the port of destination, unless such costs and charges were for the seller's account under the contract of carriage;

c) unloading costs including lighterage and wharfage charges, unless such costs and charges were for the seller's account under the contract of carriage;

d) any additional costs incurred if it fails to give notice in accordance with B7, from the agreed date or the expiry date of the agreed period for shipment, provided that the goods have been clearly identified as the contract goods; and

e) where applicable, all duties, taxes and other charges, as well as the costs of carrying out customs formalities payable upon import of the goods and the costs for their transport through any country unless included within the cost of the contract of carriage.

B7 Notices to the seller

The buyer must, whenever it is entitled to determine the time for shipping the goods and/or the point of receiving the goods within the named port of destination, give the seller sufficient notice thereof.

A8 Delivery document

The seller must, at its own expense, provide the buyer without delay with the usual transport document for the agreed port of destination.

This transport document must cover the contract goods, be dated within the period agreed for shipment, enable the buyer to claim the goods from the carrier at the port of destination and, unless otherwise agreed, enable the buyer to sell the goods in transit by the transfer of the document to a subsequent buyer or by notification to the carrier.

When such a transport document is issued in negotiable form and in several originals, a full set of originals must be presented to the buyer.

A9 Checking – packaging – marking

The seller must pay the costs of those checking operations (such as checking quality, measuring, weighing, counting) that are necessary for the purpose of delivering the goods in accordance with A4, as well as the costs of any pre-shipment inspection mandated by the authority of the country of export.

The seller must, at its own expense, package the goods, unless it is usual for the particular trade to transport the type of goods sold unpackaged. The seller may package the goods in the manner appropriate for their transport, unless the buyer has notified the seller of specific packaging requirements before the contract of sale is concluded. Packaging is to be marked appropriately.

A10 Assistance with information and related costs

The seller must, where applicable, in a timely manner, provide to or render assistance in obtaining for the buyer, at the buyer's request, risk and expense, any documents and information, including security-related information, that the buyer needs for the import of the goods and/or for their transport to the final destination.

The seller must reimburse the buyer for all costs and charges incurred by the buyer in providing or rendering assistance in obtaining documents and information as envisaged in B10.

B8 **Proof of delivery**

The buyer must accept the transport document provided as envisaged in A8 if it is in conformity with the contract.

B9 **Inspection of goods**

The buyer must pay the costs of any mandatory pre-shipment inspection, except when such inspection is mandated by the authorities of the country of export.

B10 **Assistance with information and related costs**

The buyer must, in a timely manner, advise the seller of any security information requirements so that the seller may comply with A10.

The buyer must reimburse the seller for all costs and charges incurred by the seller in providing or rendering assistance in obtaining documents and information as envisaged in A10.

The buyer must, where applicable, in a timely manner, provide to or render assistance in obtaining for the seller, at the seller's request, risk and expense, any documents and information, including security-related information, that the seller needs for the transport and export of the goods and for their transport through any country.

CIF

COST INSURANCE AND FREIGHT

CIF (insert named port of destination) Incoterms® 2010

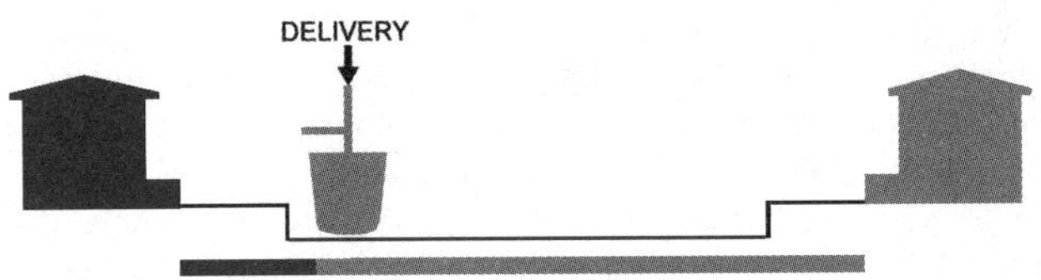

CIF

GUIDANCE NOTE

This rule is to be used only for sea or inland waterway transport.

"Cost, Insurance and Freight" means that the seller delivers the goods on board the vessel or procures the goods already so delivered. The risk of loss of or damage to the goods passes when the goods are on board the vessel. The seller must contract for and pay the costs and freight necessary to bring the goods to the named port of destination.

The seller also contracts for insurance cover against the buyer's risk of loss of or damage to the goods during the carriage. The buyer should note that under CIF the seller is required to obtain insurance only on minimum cover. Should the buyer wish to have more insurance protection, it will need either to agree as much expressly with the seller or to make its own extra insurance arrangements.

When CPT, CIP, CFR, or CIF are used, the seller fulfils its obligation to deliver when it hands the goods over to the carrier in the manner specified in the chosen rule and not when the goods reach the place of destination.

This rule has two critical points, because risk passes and costs are transferred at different places. While the contract will always specify a destination port, it might not specify the port of shipment, which is where risk passes to the buyer. If the shipment port is of particular interest to the buyer, the parties are well advised to identify it as precisely as possible in the contract.

The parties are well advised to identify as precisely as possible the point at the agreed port of destination, as the costs to that point are for the account of the seller. The seller is advised to procure contracts of carriage that match this choice precisely. If the seller incurs costs under its contract of carriage related to unloading at the specified point at the port of destination, the seller is not entitled to recover such costs from the buyer unless otherwise agreed between the parties.

The seller is required either to deliver the goods on board the vessel or to procure goods already so delivered for shipment to the destination. In addition the seller is required either to make a contract of carriage or to procure such a contract. The reference to "procure" here caters for multiple sales down a chain ('string sales'), particularly common in the commodity trades.

CIF may not be appropriate where goods are handed over to the carrier before they are on board the vessel, for example goods in containers, which are typically delivered at a terminal. In such circumstances, the CIP rule should be used.

CIF requires the seller to clear the goods for export, where applicable. However, the seller has no obligation to clear the goods for import, pay any import duty or carry out any import customs formalities.

A THE SELLER'S OBLIGATIONS

A1 General obligations of the seller

The seller must provide the goods and the commercial invoice in conformity with the contract of sale and any other evidence of conformity that may be required by the contract.

Any document referred to in A1-A10 may be an equivalent electronic record or procedure if agreed between the parties or customary.

A2 Licences, authorizations, security clearances and other formalities

Where applicable, the seller must obtain, at its own risk and expense, any export licence or other official authorization and carry out all customs formalities necessary for the export of the goods.

B THE BUYER'S OBLIGATIONS

B1 General obligations of the buyer

The buyer must pay the price of the goods as provided in the contract of sale.

Any document referred to in B1-B10 may be an equivalent electronic record or procedure if agreed between the parties or customary.

B2 Licences, authorizations, security clearances and formalities

Where applicable, it is up to the buyer to obtain, at its own risk and expense, any import licence or other official authorization and carry out all customs formalities for the import of the goods and for their transport through any country.

A3 **Contracts of carriage and insurance**

a) Contract of carriage

The seller must contract or procure a contract for the carriage of the goods from the agreed point of delivery, if any, at the place of delivery to the named port of destination or, if agreed, any point at that port. The contract of carriage must be made on usual terms at the seller's expense and provide for carriage by the usual route in a vessel of the type normally used for the transport of the type of goods sold.

b) Contract of insurance

The seller must obtain, at its own expense, cargo insurance complying at least with the minimum cover provided by Clauses (C) of the Institute Cargo Clauses (LMA/IUA) or any similar clauses. The insurance shall be contracted with underwriters or an insurance company of good repute and entitle the buyer, or any other person having an insurable interest in the goods, to claim directly from the insurer.

When required by the buyer, the seller shall, subject to the buyer providing any necessary information requested by the seller, provide at the buyer's expense any additional cover, if procurable, such as cover as provided by Clauses (A) or (B) of the Institute Cargo Clauses (LMA/IUA) or any similar clauses and/or cover complying with the Institute War Clauses and/or Institute Strikes Clauses (LMA/IUA) or any similar clauses.

The insurance shall cover, at a minimum, the price provided in the contract plus 10% (i.e., 110%) and shall be in the currency of the contract.

The insurance shall cover the goods from the point of delivery set out in A4 and A5 to at least the named port of destination.

The seller must provide the buyer with the insurance policy or other evidence of insurance cover.

Moreover, the seller must provide the buyer, at the buyer's request, risk, and expense (if any), with information that the buyer needs to procure any additional insurance.

A4 **Delivery**

The seller must deliver the goods either by placing them on board the vessel or by procuring the goods so delivered. In either case, the seller must deliver the goods on the agreed date or within the agreed period and in the manner customary at the port.

B3 **Contracts of carriage and insurance**

a) Contract of carriage

The buyer has no obligation to the seller to make a contract of carriage.

b) Contract of insurance

The buyer has no obligation to the seller to make a contract of insurance. However, the buyer must provide the seller, upon request, with any information necessary for the seller to procure any additional insurance requested by the buyer as envisaged in A3 b).

B4 **Taking delivery**

The buyer must take delivery of the goods when they have been delivered as envisaged in A4 and receive them from the carrier at the named port of destination.

A5 **Transfer of risks**

The seller bears all risks of loss of or damage to the goods until they have been delivered in accordance with A4, with the exception of loss or damage in the circumstances described in B5.

A6 **Allocation of costs**

The seller must pay

a) all costs relating to the goods until they have been delivered in accordance with A4, other than those payable by the buyer as envisaged in B6;

b) the freight and all other costs resulting from A3 a), including the costs of loading the goods on board and any charges for unloading at the agreed port of discharge that were for the seller's account under the contract of carriage;

c) the costs of insurance resulting from A3 b); and

d) where applicable, the costs of customs formalities necessary for export, as well as all duties, taxes and other charges payable upon export, and the costs for their transport through any country that were for the seller's account under the contract of carriage.

B5 **Transfer of risks**

The buyer bears all risks of loss of or damage to the goods from the time they have been delivered as envisaged in A4.

If the buyer fails to give notice in accordance with B7, then it bears all risks of loss of or damage to the goods from the agreed date or the expiry date of the agreed period for shipment, provided that the goods have been clearly identified as the contract goods.

B6 **Allocation of costs**

The buyer must, subject to the provisions of A3 a), pay

a) all costs relating to the goods from the time they have been delivered as envisaged in A4, except, where applicable, the costs of customs formalities necessary for export, as well as all duties, taxes and other charges payable upon export as referred to in A6 d);

b) all costs and charges relating to the goods while in transit until their arrival at the port of destination, unless such costs and charges were for the seller's account under the contract of carriage;

c) unloading costs including lighterage and wharfage charges, unless such costs and charges were for the seller's account under the contract of carriage;

d) any additional costs incurred if it fails to give notice in accordance with B7, from the agreed date or the expiry date of the agreed period for shipment, provided that the goods have been clearly identified as the contract goods;

e) where applicable, all duties, taxes and other charges, as well as the costs of carrying out customs formalities payable upon import of the goods and the costs for their transport through any country, unless included within the cost of the contract of carriage; and

f) the costs of any additional insurance procured at the buyer's request under A3 b) and B3 b).

A7 **Notices to the buyer**

The seller must give the buyer any notice needed in order to allow the buyer to take measures that are normally necessary to enable the buyer to take the goods.

A8 **Delivery document**

The seller must, at its own expense, provide the buyer without delay with the usual transport document for the agreed port of destination.

This transport document must cover the contract goods, be dated within the period agreed for shipment, enable the buyer to claim the goods from the carrier at the port of destination and, unless otherwise agreed, enable the buyer to sell the goods in transit by the transfer of the document to a subsequent buyer or by notification to the carrier.

When such a transport document is issued in negotiable form and in several originals, a full set of originals must be presented to the buyer.

A9 **Checking – packaging – marking**

The seller must pay the costs of those checking operations (such as checking quality, measuring, weighing, counting) that are necessary for the purpose of delivering the goods in accordance with A4, as well as the costs of any pre-shipment inspection mandated by the authority of the country of export.

The seller must, at its own expense, package the goods, unless it is usual for the particular trade to transport the type of goods sold unpackaged. The seller may package the goods in the manner appropriate for their transport, unless the buyer has notified the seller of specific packaging requirements before the contract of sale is concluded. Packaging is to be marked appropriately.

B7 **Notices to the seller**

The buyer must, whenever it is entitled to determine the time for shipping the goods and/or the point of receiving the goods within the named port of destination, give the seller sufficient notice thereof.

B8 **Proof of delivery**

The buyer must accept the transport document provided as envisaged in A8 if it is in conformity with the contract.

B9 **Inspection of goods**

The buyer must pay the costs of any mandatory pre-shipment inspection, except when such inspection is mandated by the authorities of the country of export.

A10 Assistance with information and related costs

The seller must, where applicable, in a timely manner, provide to or render assistance in obtaining for the buyer, at the buyer's request, risk and expense, any documents and information, including security-related information, that the buyer needs for the import of the goods and/or for their transport to the final destination.

The seller must reimburse the buyer for all costs and charges incurred by the buyer in providing or rendering assistance in obtaining documents and information as envisaged in B10.

B10 Assistance with information and related costs

The buyer must, in a timely manner, advise the seller of any security information requirements so that the seller may comply with A10.

The buyer must reimburse the seller for all costs and charges incurred by the seller in providing or rendering assistance in obtaining documents and information as envisaged in A10.

The buyer must, where applicable, in a timely manner, provide to or render assistance in obtaining for the seller, at the seller's request, risk and expense, any documents and information, including security-related information, that the seller needs for the transport and export of the goods and for their transport through any country.

INCOTERMS® 2010 DRAFTING GROUP

The Incoterms® 2010 rules were drafted by a select international group of ICC member experts, in consultation with the broader global ICC membership through the network of ICC national committees. The wide geographical and sectoral scope of the consultative process ensures that the Incoterms® 2010 rules reflect the current realities of international trade and respond to business needs everywhere.

CO-CHAIRS

CHARLES DEBATTISTA

Charles Debattista is an active arbitrator in international trade disputes and takes appointments under ICC and other institutional rules. He is also a Registered European Lawyer with the Bar of England and Wales and accepts instructions as counsel before international arbitral tribunals.

Mr Debattista is also a professor of Commercial Law at the University of Southampton in the UK. He has written many books and articles on international sale contracts, the carriage of goods by sea and letters of credit. He is a member of ICC's Commercial Law and Practice Commission, of the Banking Commission and of the Transport Commission. He was Chair of the Incoterms 2000 Drafting Group and Co-Chair of the Incoterms® 2010 Drafting Group.

CHRISTOPH MARTIN RADTKE

Mr Radtke is a partner of the French law firm Lamy & Associés. He leads the firm's international team and specializes in international trade law, agency and distribution, EC law, French and German business law, international arbitration, and international litigation. Admitted at the French and the German Bar, Mr Radtke has published articles on international contract law and arbitration and has taught at the Paris-based Institut de Droit Comparé. In addition to his role on the Incoterms® 2010 Drafting Group, Mr Radtke is Chair of the Commercial Law and Practice Commission of ICC France, and Vice-Chair of the French-German Lawyers' Association.

He lectures widely on the Incoterms rules and has contributed to ICC model contracts including the ICC Model Distributorship Contract and the Commercial Agency Contract, as well as to the ICC Legal Handbook on Global Sourcing Contracts.

DRAFTING GROUP MEMBERS

JENS BREDOW

Jens Bredow is the Secretary General of the German Institution of Arbitration in Cologne and an attorney in private practice, specializing in international trade law and arbitration. In addition, he serves as an adviser to the German Ministry of Justice as a participant in UNCITRAL's Working Party on Arbitration and Conciliation, and is also a lecturer at Bonn University. He is also an experienced arbitrator, serving frequently as chair or sole arbitrator in a range of international proceedings.

Mr Bredow, the former Director of ICC Germany, was also a member of the Drafting Groups that revised the Incoterms® rules in 1990 and 2000. He currently sits on the Incoterms rules Panel of Experts.

JOHNNY HERRE

Professor Johnny Herre is a Supreme Court Justice at the Supreme Court of Sweden. Prior to joining the court, he spent many years as a Professor at the Stockholm School of Economics, where he served a term as Head of the Department of Law and from which he earned a Master of Science in Economics and Business and a PhD in Law, with a focus on damages in sale of goods law.

In addition to publishing widely on issues related to the sale of goods, contracts, the law of obligations and consumer law, Professor Herre has extensive experience in arbitration, including as arbitrator and chair of tribunals in international arbitral proceedings. A member of the Study Group on a European Civil Code for many years, he is currently Chair of ICC Sweden's group on Commercial Law and Practice.

DAVID LOWE

A partner at the London office of international law firm Wragge & Co LLP, David Lowe leads the firm's commercial contracts team. His expertise is in advising supply chain clients on the international supply of goods. In this capacity, he has advised:

- international retailers on sourcing products in the Far East;
- manufacturers of industrial products on international distribution networks;
- European distributors on import arrangements with international manufacturers;
- international commodity traders ranging from bulk cement to coal;
- European manufacturers and retailers on entering new international markets; and
- international suppliers entering the European market.

Mr Lowe's experience of advising buyers and sellers of manufactured goods (which are typically transported in containers) has shaped his contribution to Incoterms® 2010. Mr Lowe also chairs the ICC UK Commercial Law and Practice Committee.

LAURI RAILAS

Lauri Railas, LL.M. (Helsinki and London), LL.D. (Helsinki), is an attorney-at-law at Krogerus Attorneys in Finland. He is a member of the Finnish Bar.

Dr Railas is the former Secretary General of ICC Finland and the former Secretary of the Arbitration Institute of the Central Chamber of Commerce of Finland. His experience and practice include international trade and transport law, marine insurance and electronic commerce. Dr Railas has been involved in trade facilitation work under the auspices of the United Nations and has written books and articles on international trade law. In addition to Incoterms® 2010, Dr Railas has contributed to various ICC model contracts, including the ICC Model International Sale Contract. He is also the Co-Chair of the ICC Task Force on Public Procurement.

FRANK REYNOLDS

Frank Reynolds is the President of International Projects Inc., a US-based international trading and consulting firm. Besides representing the US for the Incoterms® 2000 and Incoterms® 2010 revisions, he has written or co-authored 16 books on various international trade topics including ICC's *A to Z of International Trade* dictionary. He also has written over 300 columns for such international publications as the *Journal of Commerce*, *The Exporter* and ICC's *Documentary Credit Insight*.

Mr Reynolds has lectured throughout the US on such trade-related topics as the Incoterms® rules, documentary credits, US free-trade agreements, export and import procedures and the Harmonized System for over 25 years. He served on the US Commerce Department's District Export Council for 22 years, and his international projects received an *E Award for Export Excellence*. He also holds a customs broker licence from the US Department of Homeland Security, Customs and Border Protection.

MIROSLAV SUBERT

Miroslav Subert holds a *juris doctor* degree from Charles University in Prague. A long-time expert on the Incoterms® rules, he worked for many years at senior management level in companies dealing with foreign trade, shipping and forwarding in the United Kingdom, Croatia, Belgium and the Czech Republic.

Dr Subert currently serves as a lecturer at a number of institutions in Prague, including the University of Economics, the Institute for Foreign Trade, Transport and Forwarding and the Perner Institute. He is the Vice-Chair of the Czech Society for Transport Law and a professional and legal adviser on foreign trade, transport and insurance to ICC Czech Republic. He has written widely on international trade issues, including books on international transport, sales and documentary credits, and is a regular contributor to professional publications and newspapers. Dr Subert wrote a guide to Incoterms rules in 2000 and has spearheaded the translation of recent versions of the Incoterms rules into Czech.

ICC SECRETARIAT

EMILY O'CONNOR

Emily O'Connor is the Senior Policy Manager of the ICC Commission on Commercial Law and Practice and oversaw the development of *Incoterms® 2010.* She joined the ICC International Secretariat in Paris in 2006, after several years at the US Council for International Business in New York, where she managed intellectual property and competition law issues.

Ms O'Connor graduated from Columbia Law School in New York, first practising in the US State Department's Office of the Legal Adviser, focusing on International Court of Justice cases on the US application of the death penalty to foreign nationals. She then practised international corporate law at Debevoise & Plimpton, working on future flow equity issuances, mergers and acquisitions and a range of media deals, before moving to the international policy arena.

SHANE DALY

Shane Daly is a graduate of the National University of Ireland, Galway and University College London, specializing in International Commercial Law with Dispute Resolution and International Public Law. He also holds a diploma from the Université de Poitiers. In addition to his work as an assistant to the Incoterms® 2010 Drafting Group, Mr Daly has contributed to other projects of the ICC Commission on Commercial Law and Practice, including model contracts on mergers and acquisitions and on subcontracting. He is to commence as a trainee solicitor in Dublin in 2011.

ICC Dispute Resolution

Incorporating one or more of the Incoterms® rules into a contract does not in itself constitute an agreement to use ICC dispute resolution services. Contracting parties that wish to resort to one or more or these services in the event of a dispute should reach a specific and clear agreement to that effect. For this purpose, ICC offers suggested and standard clauses that parties may incorporate into their contracts. Failing this, parties should agree on the use of ICC rules in an exchange of correspondence.

ICC offers an array of services to help parties overcome disputes arising from international trade. These services respond to different needs and different situations. Each is governed by a set of rules defining a neutral procedure capable of accommodating cultural, linguistic and legal diversity, as well as the specificities of given sectors and activities.

Arbitration, administered by the ICC International Court of Arbitration, generally leads to a binding decision issued by a tribunal of one or three arbitrators. The decision is widely enforceable because of the legal recognition arbitration enjoys in almost all the world's trading nations.

Amicable dispute resolution embraces various methods of dispute resolution that seek a settlement by consensual means. The neutral third party and the parties to the dispute decide on the settlement technique to be used, which may be mediation, neutral evaluation, a mini-trial or a combination of different techniques.

Dispute boards are ongoing bodies set up for the duration of a contract to resolve disputes as and when they arise during the life of the contract. Different types of dispute boards are available, depending on the powers the parties wish to grant to the members of the board and the force of their determinations.

Expertise consists of engaging a specialist to give an opinion on a matter requiring specialist knowledge and skills, such as technical, financial or legal know-how. The services offered range from the search for a suitable expert to the complete administration of the expert's mission. A specific service called DOCDEX is offered for disputes relating to documentary credits, bank-to-bank reimbursements, collections and guarantees.

For further information, including all rules and clauses, visit our dispute resolution pages at **www.iccwbo.org**

Copyright notice and synopsis of trademark usage rules for *Incoterms® 2010*

ICC holds all copyright and other intellectual property rights in this collective work. No part of this work may be reproduced, copied, distributed, transmitted, translated or adapted in any form or by any means (whether graphic, electronic, or mechanical, and including, without limitation, photocopying, scanning, recording, taping, or by use of computer, the Internet or information retrieval systems) without the written permission of ICC through ICC Services, Publications Department.

"Incoterms" is a registered trademark of the International Chamber of Commerce.

Although ICC encourages and promotes the use of the Incoterms® rules by third parties in sales contracts in compliance with ICC's copyright policy, "Incoterms" is not a generic term that may be used to designate any trade terms, but is a trademark used to designate only the terms devised by ICC and products and services from ICC.

Below are some rules on the correct usage of the "Incoterms" trademark:

- Use the trademark "Incoterms" to refer only to ICC's Incoterms® rules and other Incoterms® products and services from ICC.
- In text, use "Incoterms" as an adjective, not a noun.
- Do not use "Incoterms" without the initial letter as a capital letter.
- Do not use "Incoterm" (without the final "s"). An individual term from the Incoterms® rules should be referred to as an Incoterms® rule, and never as an "Incoterm".
- Use the registered trademark symbol ® next to the trademark "Incoterms".
- Any use of the trademark "Incoterms" in association with products and services not from ICC requires a licence from ICC.

More information on the correct usage of ICC's "Incoterms" trademark can be found on ICC's website on the Incoterms® rules at **www.iccwbo.org/incoterms**

ICC at a glance

ICC is the world business organization, a representative body that speaks with authority on behalf of enterprises from all sectors in every part of the world.

The fundamental mission of ICC is to promote trade and investment across frontiers and help business corporations meet the challenges and opportunities of globalization. Its conviction that trade is a powerful force for peace and prosperity dates from the organization's origins early in the last century. The small group of far-sighted business leaders who founded ICC called themselves "the merchants of peace".

Because its member companies and associations are themselves engaged in international business, ICC has unrivalled authority in making rules that govern the conduct of business across borders. Although these rules are voluntary, they are observed in countless thousands of transactions every day and have become part of the fabric of international trade.

ICC also provides essential services, foremost among them the ICC International Court of Arbitration, the world's leading arbitral institution. Another service is the World Chambers Federation, ICC's worldwide network of chambers of commerce, fostering interaction and exchange of chamber best practice.

Business leaders and experts drawn from the ICC membership establish the business stance on broad issues of trade and investment policy as well as on vital technical and sectoral subjects. These include financial services, information technologies, telecommunications, marketing ethics, the environment, transportation, competition law and intellectual property.

ICC enjoys a close working relationship with the United Nations and other intergovernmental organizations, including the World Trade Organization, the G20 and the G8.

ICC was founded in 1919. Today it groups thousands of member companies and associations from over 120 countries. National committees work with their members to address the concerns of business in their countries and convey to their governments the business views formulated by ICC.

For more information, please visit **www.iccwbo.org**

Other Incoterms® 2010 products

Available in October 2010

Guide to Incoterms® 2010
By Jan Ramberg
ICC Pub. No. 720, 2010 edition
ISBN: 978-92-842-0082-5

Guide to Incoterms® 2010 by renowned expert Jan Ramberg clarifies how the Incoterms® rules work together with other terms of a contract of sale and contracts for carriage, insurance and payment.

This publication will be invaluable for all those involved in international trade: exporters, importers, lawyers, freight forwarders.

Incoterms® 2010 Wall Chart
ICC Pub. No. 716L, 2010 edition
ISBN: 978-92-842-0090-0

This practical wallchart explains all 11 Incoterms® 2010 rules at a glance, ideal for classrooms, offices or as a gift for business partners.

Incoterms® 2010
Bilingual English/French edition
ICC Pub. No. 715EF
ISBN: 978-92-842-0089-4

Bilingual editions in other languages are available from ICC national committes around the world. Please visit **www.incoterms.com** or **www.iccbooks.com** for more information.

Training

ICC Events runs training courses on the Incoterms® 2010 rules, as well as on international arbitration and negotiating international contracts for business people, corporate counsel, lawyers and legal practitioners involved in international trade.
www.iccwbo.org/events

In the banking sector

Uniform Rules for Demand Guarantees (URDG)
ICC Pub. No. 758, 2010 edition
ISBN: 978-92-842-0036-8

The ICC Uniform Rules for Demand Guarantees (URDG), first adopted in 1991, reflect international standard practice in the use of demand guarantees. Further, they balance the legitimate interests of all parties. Since their adoption, the URDG have gained international acceptance and official recognition by bankers, traders, industry associations and international organizations including UNCITRAL, FIDIC and the World Bank.

Also available in French-English (bilingual edition)

Order at www.iccbooks.com

ICC publications for global business

ICC's list of specialized publications covers a range of topics including international banking, international trade reference and rules (the Incoterms® rules), law and arbitration, counterfeiting and fraud, model commercial contracts and environmental issues.

ICC products are available from ICC national committees, which exist in over 90 countries around the world. Contact details for a national committee in your country are available at **www.iccwbo.org**

You may also order ICC products online from the ICC Business Bookstore at **www.iccbooks.com,** or purchase them at the ICC Secretariat, located at the address below.

The world business organisation

ICC United Kingdom
12 Grosvenor Place
London, SW1X 7HH
United Kingdom
Tel. +44 20 7838 9363
Fax. +44 20 7235 5447
e-mail publications@iccorg.co.uk

International Chamber of Commerce

The world business organization

ICC Publications
38 Cours Albert 1er
75008 Paris
France
Tel. +33 1 49 53 29 23
Fax. +33 1 49 53 29 02
e-mail pub@iccwbo.org